Latin America in the Twenty-First Century: Toward a New Sociopolitical Matrix

LATIN AMERICA IN THE TWENTY-FIRST CENTURY:
TOWARD A NEW SOCIOPOLITICAL MATRIX

Manuel Antonio Garretón
Marcelo Cavarozzi
Peter S. Cleaves
Gary Gereffi
Jonathan Hartlyn

North·South Center Press
UNIVERSITY OF MIAMI

The publisher of this book is the North-South Center Press at the University of Miami.

The mission of the North-South Center is to promote better relations and serve as a catalyst for change among the United States, Canada, and the nations of Latin America and the Caribbean by advancing knowledge and understanding of the major political, social, economic, and cultural issues affecting the nations and peoples of the Western Hemisphere.

All copyright inquiries should be addressed to the publisher: North-South Center Press, 1500 Monza Avenue, Coral Gables, Florida 33146-3027, U.S.A., phone 305-284-8912, fax 305-284-5089, or e-mail mmapes@nsc.msmail.miami.edu.

To order or to return books, contact Lynne Rienner Publishers, Inc., 1800 30th Street, Suite 314, Boulder, CO 80301-1026, 303-444-6684, fax 303-444-0824.

Library of Congress Cataloging-in-Publication Data

Garretón Merino, Manuel A. (Manuel Antonio)
Latin America in the twenty-first century: toward a new sociopolitical matrix / Manuel Antonio Garretón ... [et al.].
p. cm.
Includes bibliographical references and index.
ISBN 1-57454-106-4 (hc: alk. paper) — ISBN 1-57454-104-8 (pbk: alk. paper)
1. Latin America—Social conditions. 2. Latin America—Politics and government. 3. Latin America—Economic conditions. 4. Latin America—Economic policy. 5. Latin America—Social policy. 6. Globalization. I. Title.

HN110.5.A8G335 2003
306'.098—dc21   2003048706

Printed in the United States of America/TS

08 07 06 05 04 03   6 5 4 3 2 1

Contents

ACKNOWLEDGMENTS

This book began as a set of joint reflections building on the valuable papers and ensuing debate that took place at a Conference on "Rethinking Development Theories in Latin America: Democratic Governance, Processes of Globalization and Societal Transformations," held at the University of North Carolina at Chapel Hill in March 1993. This conference was made possible by a generous grant from The Dante B. Fascell North-South Center of the University of Miami, as well as by supplementary funding from the College of Arts and Sciences at UNC-Chapel Hill and from the Working Group on Political and Economic Regimes of the Consortium in Latin American Studies at the University of North Carolina at Chapel Hill and Duke University. Further fruitful discussions were held at the University of Salamanca in Spain in June 1994, which were supported by funds from the Comisión Interministerial de Ciencia y Tecnología (CICYT) and coordinated through the Asociación de Investigación y Especialización sobre Temas Iberoamericanos (AIETI). We are particularly grateful to Manuel Alcántara, Guadalupe Ruiz-Giménez, Christian L. Freres, and Raúl Morodó for providing us with several stimulating intellectual venues within which we could discuss our ideas with our Spanish colleagues, as well as with generous hospitality. Subsequent drafts were discussed and debated over the years at multiple conventions of the Latin American Studies Association. We made our final revisions, including updates where they were needed, in late fall 2002 and winter 2003.

This book is a collective enterprise. Building on sections initially authored by each of us, Manuel Antonio Garretón wrote a first draft, drawing in part upon some of his previous works published elsewhere, and Jonathan Hartlyn coordinated the final revision of the manuscript. We are particularly grateful to the contributors of papers to the 1993 conference, a number of which were published as a special issue of *Síntesis: Revista de Ciencias Sociales Iberoamericanas* (Madrid), no. 22 (July-December, 1994). The authors of these papers included Renato Boschi, Michael Coppedge, Alvaro Díaz, Carlos Filgueira, Evelyne Huber, Guillermo O'Donnell, Ricardo Ffrench-Davis, Roberto Bouzas, Blanca Torres, and Alain Touraine. Similarly valuable presentations or comments were made by Carol Wise and Julio Labastida. The ideas presented in these papers provided a crucial initial springboard for our own thoughts regarding what is an appropriate framework to understand contemporary change in the region, which have come together in this volume. We also thank Kenneth Roberts and Phillip Mauceri, the two outside reviewers for the North-South Center Press, for their valuable comments. At various stages of this project, Eduardo Feldman, Mary Alice McCarthy, Scott Graves, and Merike Blofield provided excellent research assistance. With gratitude we acknowledge the support and tolerance displayed by our spouses and partners as we took time from family and friends to complete this project.

Finally, we would like to thank William C. Smith at the University of Miami for his continuous encouragement and Kathleen Hamman of the North-South Center Press for her superb editorial assistance. We also wish to thank Mary Mapes for designing the cover and formatting the book, Susan Holler for creating the index, and Michelle Perez for proofreading the text.

INTRODUCTION

L atin American countries have departed from an old style of politics and are moving, albeit irregularly, to new political forms, structures, and governing patterns that are closely tied to observable changes in these nations' economies and societies. In the pages that follow, we present and employ the term "sociopolitical matrix" (SPM) to capture the relevant factors underlying these relationships. In doing so, we concur with those who espouse the need to move from grand paradigms to middle-level hypotheses; from unicausal and unidirectional theories to the study of inter-related processes; and from understanding change as a form of essentialist determinism between structures to reciprocal historical causation across economic, political, social, and cultural dimensions. Thus, we envision the need to rethink "development theories" about the region and the nature of Latin American development itself.

If generalizing about Latin America as a whole was always problematic, it is now becoming increasingly so. It is particularly insufficient to specify a determined state of affairs (usually in a typology) and then to ascertain which countries fall into which categories. We are no longer in a position, and perhaps never will be again, to define a single Latin American problematique, as was done earlier around concepts such as "development," "revolution," "dependency," "modernization," and "democratization." These terms described a central challenge these countries faced and granted the observer the liberty of papering over the countries' diversity by concentrating not on each country but on the challenge. Latin American countries were presented as differing only in the degree to which they experienced, say, development, revolutions, or democracies.

Today, diverse processes related to economic development, political and social democratization, and cultural models of modernity are occurring simultaneously and are fundamentally intertwined, but their relationship is neither always causal or immutable.[1] Scholars must abandon the notion that a single paradigm of causal relationships somehow exists, which was a characteristic of some social analysis in previous decades. The relationship among diverse processes is empirical, historical, and can be set out theoretically only if abstract determinism and reductionism are avoided. That is, each of these processes has its own dynamic and its own actors, and the relationships among the processes and their outcomes are not scripted in definitive form. Rather, the outcomes depend on the actors and forces involved.

Our argument, in simplified form, is that major Latin American countries approximated what we call the "statist-national-popular SPM" from the 1930s to the 1980s. Features of the international economy and geopolitics were determinant during the emergence of this sociopolitical matrix and maintained their prominence during its heyday. Beginning in the 1970s, external changes and internal tensions led to a gradual decomposition of the matrix, in irregular and sometimes wretched twists, leading to, at best, partial and uneven recomposition. A potential future SPM should incorporate strategies for political management, economic expansion, social integration, and cultural expression. While not yet clearly delineated, several of its features are in evidence, which will be discussed below. The various processes, which differ in their content and evolution in each country, emerge in a world context entirely different from the one prevalent a half century ago, when the historical *problematique* contrasted "Western" development with "non-Western" underdevelopment.

Our analysis is organized in the following way. In Chapter One, we present the concept of sociopolitical matrix — whose basic elements include a state, a political system of representation, a socioeconomic base of social actors and cultural relations, all mediated by a political regime — and an affinity to middle-range theorizing. In Chapter Two, we discuss the previous matrix that was dominant particularly in the larger Latin American countries, which we term "statist-national-popular." We discuss its theoretical underpinnings, its antecedents, and its basic elements. Chapter Three presents major features of the new world context, particularly with regard to how globalization and its economic effects impact the region, and ends with a section that examines past patterns of relations between the region and the world economy. Chapter Four then examines the most significant political, social, and cultural challenges that have resulted in Latin America as a consequence of the interaction between global and domestic contexts. Subsequently, in Chapter Five, we analyze key trends in the emerging development model and in associated state, polity, and sociocultural spheres that highlight the decomposition of the previous sociopolitical matrix and the tendencies that would shape a potential future one. As trends remain inchoate, it is difficult to distinguish what may be temporary transition phenomena from longer-lasting processes. In our concluding chapter, we discuss major possible future directions for the region, arguing that efforts to build a market-driven matrix have failed, while considering the difficulties in moving from the current disjointed reality to a new multicentered matrix, which could be more propitious for human development in the region.

Chapter One

SOCIOPOLITICAL MATRIX

S ocial scientists studying Latin America in the recent past generally have tried to create middle-range approaches and theories on development in the region, so that the literature encompasses 1) the construction of political democracy, 2) social integration, 3) regional insertion into the world economy, and 4) the search for modernity.[2] These basic processes define the major contemporary set of issues for the Latin American region or its *problematique*. What we seek to provide in these pages are a conceptual framework and tools within which this kind of theorizing can be further advanced.

In our view, these many middle-range theories and approaches have emerged as a reaction against excessively global theories or paradigms of development, built around master concepts such as modernization or dependency. The main axes of these global theories of development were economic, even if their proponents conceded that development had social, political, or cultural dimensions. These general theories of development were found to be unsatisfactory, even with regard to the reality they were purporting to describe, and are even more unsuitable for providing a basis for explaining current trends and processes. The contemporary alternative global theory of development, neoliberalism, is also characterized by the defects of the older theories or paradigms. These include excessive globalism, careless generalization, disciplinary narrowness, and reductionist thinking. Neoliberalism also suffers from economic determinism that acts as an ideology justifying the imposition by governments of orthodox economic principles on their people.

Recent trends in political science around certain rational choice or neoinstitutionalist approaches provide alternative risks of seeking to provide explanations for socioeconomic and political changes that are excessively narrow, decontextualizing the political sphere and separating it from the socioeconomic reality within which it is embedded. Although there are many excellent examples of such work that have advanced our understanding, in some cases work in this tradition provides incomplete and unsatisfactory answers, due to a focus on formalism over content or to its own type of reductionism and narrow disciplinary focus, eschewing necessary consideration of the crucial role played by historical context and interactive dynamics with other spheres of social life.[3]

Thus, we situate our work within the tradition of middle-range theories, joining them in avowedly rejecting structural overdetermination. At the same time, through the concept of sociopolitical matrix (SPM), we intend to provide a means through which analysis of both the autonomy and the interconnections of political, state, socioeconomic, and cultural spheres can proceed, in this way also avoiding the alternative risk of excessive decontextualization. By beginning with a concept such as sociopolitical matrix, we believe we can understand the set of processes relating to development in a more comprehensive and less teleological manner. The concept of sociopolitical matrix provides a way to study social and political change in Latin America in a more integrated fashion than is true of other prevalent approaches to date. An SPM refers to relationships among the state, a structure for representation or a political party system (to aggregate global demands and involve subjects politically), and a socioeconomic base of social actors with cultural orientations and relations (including the participation and diversity of civil society outside formal state structures) — all mediated institutionally by the political regime.

Although this conceptualization will be further elaborated below, at this point it may be useful to clarify how we view the state and the political regime. The state is the set of public institutions with integrating and coercive functions, also known as a development agent, a crystallization of domination, and a symbolic projection of unity. The state is not viewed here as a mere agent of domination that needs to be destroyed or conquered and controlled. Nor is the proper concept that of a neutral instrument, decoupled from the country's history, made up of institutions and organizations at the service of a technocratic elite. On one side, the state combines symbolic and concrete institutions, instruments, actors, and agents that are relatively autonomous. On the other side, it exercises coercive, regulatory, redistributive, and integrative functions, depending on the sphere of society with which it interacts. What this means is that the state is simultaneously the factor that unifies a historical society called a nation, a development agent, an instrument with coercive functions, a set of relations of domination, and an organizational apparatus and public institution charged with these functions. The state's functions cannot be reduced to any one of these singular dimensions, although in specific historical moments the state may be linked more to one or some of them than to others.

It is useful to distinguish between "stateness" and "statism." When we refer to stateness in this book, we refer to state principles and functions, such as consensus building, national unity, agreement on fundamentals, the territorial integrity of the nation, or the constitution. These are all distinguished from statism, by which we mean significant government policies, such as those establishing the state's extensive intervention in the market. And, as will be discussed below, in different historical periods there may be an apparent importance of one over the other, though effective development requires both stateness and statism.

A "political regime" describes an institutional pattern of governance, that is, how people link with the state (whether as citizens, clients, or in a completely subordinated fashion) and how demands and social conflict are processed. In this sense, democracy is not a type of society but strictly a type of political regime, characterized by certain ethical principles and specific mechanisms (such as popular suffrage, rule of law, human rights, alternation of elected leaders, political and ideological pluralism, and deconcentrated power). Thus, democracy as a political regime can evolve independently from the other spheres of the SPM, even as it is also related to them.

SPM analysis deals with the most general characteristics of social transformation from a perspective that pays special attention to the constitution of social actors and their historical actions. To explain this in another way, a society defines itself not just by its economy, its social structure, its culture, or its politics, but by all of them. The crisscrossing of these dimensions constitutes what we call the society's SPM. The concept seeks to be a nexus between simple description and abstract theory about these societies. It is not precisely a theory from which one can deduce a singular hypothesis or rule for relations across spheres, because diverse hypotheses can be advanced to explain the evolution and characteristics of a determined SPM, and we will propose that certain ones fit certain kinds of SPMs better than others. The SPM is better described as a heuristic instrument, as a tool that can be employed analytically to aid in understanding broad historical tendencies in Latin America. Some might believe it more appropriate to speak of several competing matrices within any given national society taken as an analytical unit, rather than a single matrix. For the sake of simplification, we refer to a dominant matrix (whether consolidated, failed, or inchoate), which is more akin to an ideal type that never existed perfectly in reality, rather than to a precise empirical set of relations that applies equally well to all cases.

We should underscore at this point that the concept begins with the assumption of historical societies denominated as nations and understood to operate as states. At the same time, the concept permits analysis of the possibility that certain current trends are significantly redefining notions of the territoriality of societies and the sense of nationhood, impacting sovereignty.

SPMs, which emerge, consolidate, and eventually decompose, are analytically interesting when they have a prolonged life span. The fact of persevering for a relatively long time indicates that the various components are mutually reinforcing and self-sustaining. Since the mid-nineteenth century, more than one SPM can be identified in large Latin American countries, and several derivatives or subsets in smaller or less autonomous nations. SPMs capable of reproducing themselves over several generations can be identified, as they encompass mutually reinforcing strategies for economic growth, social integration, political representation, and cultural expression. Consolidated SPMs advance a sufficient number of interests and aspirations to achieve relative social peace internally and at least some minimal degree of autonomy externally to prolong the experiment. The sociopolitical matrix most prevalent in the region until the contemporary period of change, particularly among the larger countries, was the statist-national-popular sociopolitical matrix.[4] In turn, SPMs in decomposition are evident from the fact that they experience "exhaustion" of the growth strategy, "disarticulation" of social identities, "delegitimation" of the representational strategy, and "rejection" of canons of cultural expression.

The dynamic interactions of the diverse components of an SPM are known as political processes. Of the many possible political processes, we are especially interested in those that relate to a crisis or a sharpening of contradictions in a certain time period, principally referring to changes in the political regime, to the breakdown of democratic practices, or to political democratization. However, crisis and regime change in the last two decades highlight a more dramatic and profound modification in the type of society, in the forms of collective action, that is, in the sociopolitical matrix. Suggestive of the depth of transformations have been the frequency of democratic collapses, the severity of authoritarian regimes, and the resiliency of democratic transitions, especially faced with drastic economic adjustments and changes in the development model.

Thus, in order to understand the likelihood of sustainability or transformation of a given sociopolitical matrix, it is important to consider issues closely linked to the entire web of relations, such as between the development model and new international currents, between the social base and social movements, between representation and social democratization, and between the cultural dimension and views regarding modernity.

Development should not be confused with a mode of production, such as industrial, or a model of accumulation, like capitalism. Nor is it coterminous with a particular instrument, such as the market, or the state, or a certain growth strategy, or insertion within the international scene like the open economy. A development model is all these elements within a determined historical context. Thus, by development model, we mean a vision and practice that articulates economic growth and social change; assigning roles to the state and to domestic economic agents; assuming a patterned relationship with the international environment; attracting popular support because of its normative, affective, or ideological persuasiveness; and providing for its own evolution.

For our purposes, there is also a difference between an economic model and a development model. An economic model has a narrower focus on a generally defined set of relationships among factors of production (for example, capital, labor, material resources, and technology), which lead to differing patterns of output of goods and services, employment, and investment. The economic model does not take into account all the other elements that we consider parts of a development model, especially social and political dimensions. Development models permeate political debate, economic policy, the decisions of private business, and the expectations of the citizenry. Opposing political and economic actors compete over the definition of the development model because the definition determines who controls decisionmaking and the allocation of goods and services under the model's auspices.

A development model's equation for economic growth must have the support of a coalition. The model's proponents must also legitimize it to some extent among those who are not its immediate or direct beneficiaries. To be self-sustaining, the model needs flexible and adaptable strategies for growth that allow its renovation and reproduction (in this sense, structural adjustments constitute a strategy and not a development model). A new growth strategy could mean the renovation of a development model but could also lead to its replacement, especially when economic stagnation is severe, one or more factors of production are severely underutilized, and political legitimacy is weak. Circumstances such as these facilitate, indeed, necessitate the emergence of a new approach that takes hold by exploiting idle or inefficient labor and capital or material resources, by promising benefits with widespread appeal, and by acquiring the backing of groups not wedded to the previous model. When the growth strategy atrophies or no longer generates sufficient surplus or when its benefits are no longer apparent to relevant groups, the development model falters, leading to social and political unrest. Often the coalition behind the initially successful model refuses to sacrifice over the short term to help insure its long-term sustainability. Thus, the more closed and unified the coalition behind the model, the less likely its key features will evolve and adapt to new economic and technological challenges. A development model will perpetuate itself to the degree that it contains mechanisms within its intrinsic logic permitting self-correction and to the degree that it is based on a flexible coalition that admits entry of new groups.

Also relevant to understanding the evolution of a given sociopolitical matrix or the likelihood of its change are social movements. Social movements are defined as types of collective actions that have relative stability over time and a certain degree of organization, oriented toward change or conservation of some sphere of social life. From one perspective, *social movements* (lower case and plural) are forms of collective action that respond to and try to resolve specific tensions or contradictions. From another perspective, a *Social Movement* (SM, capitalized and singular) is a carrier of a sense of history and the incarnation of a force for broad social change. Social movements consist of concrete actors oriented toward specific goals and, thus, must be specified in each society and historical moment. They maintain problematic relations with other social movements, and when they are sufficiently pervasive in a society, two or more social movements may together constitute an SM. For example, the feminist movement in Brazil in the 1970s was a social movement that was part of the democratization Social Movement. In analyzing political processes, it is useful to distinguish social movements, which are a type of collective action, from other important forms of social action relating to regime change, such as demands and mobilizations. Also, it should be emphasized that a Social Movement does not necessarily appear in every historical period.

Another important concept is modernity, which we define here as a society's capacity to construct its own fate (history) through reason, subjectivity, and memory. In contrast, when history is considered to be predestined, determined by tradition, by nature, or inevitably imposed by others, the society is pre-modern. Modernity is the way that subjects affirm themselves, combining rational, instrumental, expressive, and symbolic dimensions. For example, a group that believes its success depends on the gods would be pre-modern, whereas one that tries to mold its own situation would be modern. The identity of a people or group can be purposefully constructed (modern), or it can be defined by others (pre-modern); at the same time, all identities are filtered through historical memory.

This notion of modernity is crucial for illuminating new types of socio-historical action. Under the old statist-national-popular SPM, one concept of modernity (Western) and one strategy (industrialization) were dominant. The identities were based on work, production, state, and class. One characteristic we see in contemporary Latin America under the potentially emergent SPM is that there are diverse modernities, yet one is not wholly dominant. Identities are based variously on gender, ethnicity, region, language, advocacy, economic activity, and antisocial or rebellious behavior, all of which are seeking space in a new SPM.

Chapter Two

CHARACTERISTICS OF THE STATIST-NATIONAL-POPULAR SOCIOPOLITICAL MATRIX

THE BASIC ELEMENTS

An ideal type by definition cannot cover all particular cases, even though it might describe a situation shared to a greater or lesser degree by most Latin American countries. In describing the statist-national-popular SPM, we would tend to exclude those countries that remained under oligarchic domination — particularly the predominantly Central American and Caribbean late-late modernizers — and that only belatedly incorporated traces of the statist-national-popular matrix, even as it was fading as a relatively stable model.

The principal characteristic of any SPM is the relative interdependence among its components, that is, the state, political parties, and various social actors, all reinforced by economic relations and ideology. In turn, a central feature of the statist-national-popular SPM especially present in the larger countries of Latin America was the fact that several of its components were relatively fused. The autonomy of each component was weak, and the combination of two or three tended to suppress or to impose on the others. The particular combination of domination and subordination depended on historical factors and varied from country to country. The major elements of the statist-national-popular SPM are presented in Table 1.

This statist-national-popular SPM prevailed from the 1930s through the early 1980s. The Mexican case revealed a fusion between the state and the Institutional Revolutionary Party (Partido Revolucionario Institucional — PRI) that absorbed civil society. In the Argentine case, social actors projected themselves directly into the state through a pattern of segmented colonization, overriding the system of representation through forms of *caudillismo* (personalistic, unaccountable, clientelistic strong-man rule). In Brazil, in partial contrast, the state remained somewhat stronger than the social actors, and traditional forms of representation sustained themselves. The Chilean and Uruguayan cases were characterized by the layering of political parties and social actors pressuring the state institutionally in the midst of a weak civil society. Like these two countries, Colombia had similarly stronger parties and selected social actors but in a context of an even weaker state and of more marginalized popular sectors, placing it more at the edge of the ideal type than the previous cases.

In the statist-national-popular SPM, the state as a symbol and institution of unity played a central role, both in its functions to assign resources via social and redistributive policies and to articulate social demands. In the majority of cases, the most effective form of collective action was directly political (mobilizational). The weakest part of the SPM was the absence of well-established institutional relations among its various components, that is, its weakest part was its political regime, whether it was democratic or authoritarian. Inward-looking economic growth, industrial modernization, national autonomy, and social integration of the middle class and organized popular sectors also characterized the statist-national-popular SPM.[5] Social action was subordinated to politics, which was expressed in a strengthening of mobilized political actors irrespective of their degree of representation. People favored collective action when they wanted to press social demands, as long as that collective action was organized and politically oriented.

THE DEVELOPMENT MODEL

The economic strategy of the statist-national-popular SPM was inward-looking, characterized by import substitution and an important role for the state. This approach advocated pursuing economic growth by manufacturing products domestically that previously had been imported, assumed more equitable income distribution derived from economic growth, and was accompanied by social and cultural policies consistent with the economic model.

Numerous Latin American countries experienced booms in the last quarter of the nineteenth century based on commodity exports, facilitated by the construction of railroads and ports during that period. Latin American governments borrowed abroad to help pay for this infrastructure, creating debt service obligations that were retired from export earnings. Through World War I and the 1920s, exports were sufficient to stimulate the local economy and service the debt. Earnings from coffee, cattle, and grain permitted domestic savings and local capital formation that were channeled in part to nascent industrialization, frequently led by European immigrants. Indeed, industrialization in Latin America began in Brazil and Argentina prior to deliberate state policies promoting industrial growth. This industrialization was an extension of the production of commodity products in forward and backward linkages and thrived to the extent that the local economy could add value to the commodity product prior to export. Until the 1930s, the motor of Latin American economies continued to be exports. The most powerful economic elites were exporters of agricultural products; industrialists, when not also agricultural exporters as individuals, were second-level producers.

Table 1. The Statist-National-Popular Sociopolitical Matrix

Characteristics	*Prevalent from 1930s to 1980s*
Sociopolitical Matrix	**Statist-National-Popular**
Components: state, political system of representation, socioeconomic base of social actors, cultural relations, mediated by political regime	Relative fusion among several components suppressing or imposing on others, weak autonomy, predominance of the state and politics.
Development Model	National industrialization, with a progressive motivating vision of the future and a strong role for the state.
International Economy	Import substitution industrialization model, at odds with dominant world trend.
Civil Society, Actors/Subjects	Actors based primarily on work, production, state, class, and politics.
Ideology, Cultural Orientation	Nationalist, populist, modernizing, politically centered, fused.
Political System of Representation	Fused with other components, a "compromise state" with a hybrid political regime or oscillating between democratic and authoritarian, weak institutionalization and high capacity of mobilization of political actors.
Concept of Modernity	Western, industrial model, identities predominantly around national state, politics and classes, invoking "the people," predominance of middle class values, absence or subordination of ethnic identities.
Role of the State	Maintain control over national territory, articulate the national development model, carry out extensive management of the economy, highly visible role for statism, main referent for collective action.
Vulnerabilities/Risks	Fiscal deficits, trade imbalance, excessive subordination of productive forces to politics, erratic and inconsistent public policies, failure to redistribute, dependence on foreign capital, and ideological polarization.

The late nineteenth century also witnessed a worldwide consensus on the value of education, which was the deus ex machina for spreading the benefits of national wealth to all sectors. In a burst of progressivist inspiration, Latin American elites founded scientific institutions, professional associations, and hospitals as expressions of national modernity, simulating comparable developments in Europe.[6] These new institutions enjoyed state recognition and some public financial support. The role of the state, however, was limited, even in education. The Catholic Church, despite secularization and pressure on its wealth and prerogatives, remained the national institution primarily responsible for the poor. In the late nineteenth and early twentieth centuries, the political challenge was to integrate the middle class into institutional politics, and the development strategy attracted support from these groups even as they competed with the traditional oligarchy for increased political influence. The working class was small, and in most countries workers were not yet a significant factor in national politics, despite their incipient organization and dramatic confrontations with factory and mining owners and with the police and army over labor grievances.

The Great Depression in the United States and Europe resulted in reduced demand for Latin American commodities, lower agricultural prices, and balance of payments crises. Economic stress led to political unrest, and military governments replaced civilian regimes in many countries. To confront the foreign exchange shortage, Latin American governments made it more difficult for the private sector to import goods and to export capital. Governments instituted high tariffs and import quotas, introduced exchange controls, and continued to devalue their currencies; many defaulted on international loans. Latin America's links to the international economy atrophied, as trade declined precipitously and capital inflows ceased. Many consumer and industrial goods, previously imported, simply were not available, creating a demand filled by new industrialists who could gain access to investment capital to produce these goods.

This trend toward greater industrial capacity was pushed along by skewed market conditions, international isolation, and entrepreneurial opportunism, rather than being a deliberate national strategy. Early stage industrialization did not have a systematic state policy, a coalition of social forces with a stated mission, or a legitimizing ideology. In strict terms, it was not a national development strategy but a reactive one. During the 1930s, however, a coalition for import substitution was beginning to take shape. The Mexican and Brazilian governments explicitly wooed urban workers with populist rhetoric and policies, while channeling their organizational energies into state-controlled unions. New industrialists looked to the state for loans to expand their operations and for controlling workers' demands. State economic intervention became progressively more sophisticated and included agencies, such as Chile's Corporation for the Promotion of Production (Corporación de Fomento de la Producción — CORFO), founded in 1939, and Mexico's National Financial Institution (Nacional Financiera — NAFINSA), with specific goals of state ownership of firms and industrial promotion.

World War II gave a new push to Latin American industrialization. Demand increased for Latin American agricultural and mineral exports. The availability of capital goods imports from Europe and the United States declined because of the mobilization of their economies for the war effort (Asia was not a player at the time). Once again, the Latin American economies generated a demand for industrial products, which a growing industrial sector could fill with only limited competition from imports. The results were impressive. Whereas in 1939 in Brazil, for example, the percent of gross national product (GNP) represented by industrialization was 14.5 percent, the figure rose to 21.2 percent by 1950.[7] Latin America had the first newly industrializing countries (NICs), principally Brazil, Mexico, Argentina, and Chile.

These economic changes brought about shifts in the class composition of Latin American societies. The industrial elite began to distinguish itself from the old agricultural oligarchy and articulated interests that were clearly contrary to agricultural exporters, such as tariff protection. Agricultural elites began to lose at least some of their traditional political clout, culminating in Chile, Colombia, and Peru with agrarian reforms in the 1960s and 1970s that had mixed results. The national capitals and regional cities attracted increasing numbers of migrants to service and factory jobs. Peasants became workers, and their proximity to the centers of national power made them open to union recruitment and political party proselytizing. The surge of democratic enthusiasm after World War II gave considerable degrees of freedom to political organizers, and the electoral participation of popular groups (if not their autonomy) increased markedly. In sum, industrialists and workers were groups to be reckoned with. The political class needed a development and governing model appropriate for this new correlation of forces.

A key event was the 1949 publication of Raúl Prebisch's manifesto that established a theoretical justification for a push toward industrialization.[8] Prebisch's argument was that Latin America suffered declining terms of trade for its agricultural exports compared with industrial imports. Industrialization, furthermore, was more effective in generating and absorbing technology and increasing labor productivity. It behooved Latin America to devise a deliberate strategy for industrialization to close the gap with richer nations. The natural first step was to substitute national industrialization for imported products. Prebisch's thoughts were of course more complex than this; he insisted that for the model to work, parallel conditions needed to be achieved, for example, in agricultural modernization. Nonetheless, Prebisch's approach emanated from his position at the United Nations' Economic Commission for Latin America

(ECLA),[9] and import substitution industrialization (ISI) became the dominant economic policy for most large Latin American countries during the next two decades.

A corollary of ISI was a more active economic role for state agencies. Traditionally low domestic savings throughout these societies and a tendency for Latin American economic elites to deposit their savings abroad meant that private capital available for industrialization was scarce. Latin American states filled the breach through public credit to private industrialists and frequently by the creation of state industries. By way of nationalization, expropriations, or new public enterprises, Latin American states became the owners of utilities, transport companies, petroleum and mining concerns, banks, steel companies, and a host of manufacturing concerns. Other investments — particularly in consumer goods and automobiles — came from large multinational firms eager to access these protected domestic markets, which were typically barred from ownership of key industries such as petroleum extraction. The dynamic growth of the state sector was almost always advantageous to domestic industrial elites because they obtained subsidized credit and were often charged low prices for public utility services (water and electricity). Thus, they influenced the state in setting controlled prices, which virtually assured manufacturers a profit margin.[10] This strategy also evolved very much to the benefit of those elements of the urban workforce in large industries, because they acquired well-paid jobs and held leadership posts in the mostly state-guided unions.

Policies similar in nature though not in scope to those of some of the European welfare states filled out the development strategy. The expectation was that industrialization brought national wealth and that this wealth should be distributed indirectly to the population at large through government programs. Public education moved steadily toward universal coverage. National health systems provided adequate service for the growing middle class and for workers organized in leading industries. Food subsidies on high consumption items contributed to industrialization by making life affordable for large segments of the popular classes despite low wages. These programs were designed to improve the quality of life for the citizenry and to generate widespread support for the development strategy in general. A number of them were available to all citizens, including members of the middle class who arguably could pay for health, education, and food without a state subsidy.

The development model was not complete, however, without an ideological dimension. In post-war Latin America, nationalism bonded together disparate classes, regions, and cultural groups. Nationalism in each country represented different mixes of cultural uniqueness, protection of economic interests, and cohesion in defense of the national territory. At a subnational level, collectivist attitudes were propagated in labor, peasant, and urban movements. Leaders of the popular sectors stressed subrogating individual aspirations to the collective good. Nationalism and collective orientations were part of the state's objective of nation-building, in order to create common identity among the rapidly growing and differentiating populations, foster allegiance to the governing system, and secure compliance with the dictates of authority. Nationalism permeated political discourse, the educational system, foreign policy, and even import substitution industrialization. ISI and post-war Latin American nationalism were mutually supportive. High tariff barriers discouraged foreign imports and elevated the status of domestic products. Barriers to foreign investment set boundaries between *lo nacional* (that which is domestic) and *lo extranjero* (that which is foreign). Expropriations energized citizens with their nation's power to stand up to foreign interests. Scenes of molten metal, hydroelectric plants, and jet airliners with national emblems taking off spurred patriotism and a belief that one's country was in the same league as more advanced industrialized countries. Domestic industrial elites were nationalistic in part because the sentiment reinforced arguments for protection against foreign competition. Nationalism also contributed to labor discipline; union organizers, especially those inspired by Marxism-Leninism, more often than not pointed to U.S. interests as the enemy rather than domestic capitalists.

Over the period from the 1950s through the 1970s, the economic component of the strategy took somewhat different forms in each of the major countries. Mexico, for example, emphasized protective tariffs for basic industries; extensive state investments in steel, petroleum, agriculture, and energy; and tight monetary policy to control inflation. A managed electoral system and deliberate suspicion of the United States underpinned the strategy, which favored the political class, industrialists, and segments of labor. Brazil exploited the model to pursue very rapid growth, with the accent on achieving a modest industrial export capability. The role of the state in the economy was larger than elsewhere, especially in credit and subsidies, and the military was part of the governing coalition for an extended period. High growth camouflaged — and Brazilian nationalism blurred — the inequitable distribution of benefits that the model generated. The Chilean model was among the more statist in the region, with the public sector playing a crucial role in finance and regulation and as a direct investor in many key industries. Colombia adopted a less extreme version of ISI, with lower average tariff rates, a more tolerant attitude toward foreign investment, greater restraint in subsidies and public credits, and a preference for joint ventures rather than wholly owned state industries.

The ISI model had a number of inherent tensions and limitations, whose importance grew over time. Among the economic flaws in the model was the lack of incentives to invent and apply new technology in ever more efficient industrial uses. While Latin American scientists authored technological innovations, commercial imperatives did not exist for companies in the local market to utilize them because these markets were noncompetitive. Nor were there many commercial reasons for these economies to legislate protection for intellectual property, and they did not. The result was that most technological innovations continued to occur abroad and be imported — even Latin American inventions were patented and commercialized in industrialized countries. Another problem was the limited proportion of the workforce that could be employed in industry. While growth in employment and income was high during the initial spurt of import substitution, the economies' inability to graduate to more sophisticated levels of production, for example, capital goods industries, halted the momentum toward employment generation. Increased state control over the economy led to overregulation, especially as decrees caused unintended consequences, which authorities tried to correct with more decrees. The complex, far-reaching and overlapping regulations eventually created an enforcement problem for the state. Evasion was relatively simple, and low-level state bureaucrats found they could exchange selective enforcement for bribes to supplement their salaries.

The welfare state precepts of the model created increasing burdens on state agencies and the private sector. Spurred by idealism, legislatures and state ministries committed the state to provide education, health coverage, and employment protection for large segments of the population. The economy failed to generate sufficient surpluses to fuel needed investments, satisfy consumption demands, and fund social programs — which invariably were neglected, especially given the elites' penchant to save and invest abroad.

The results of social policy were twofold. First, many more Latin Americans, especially those with low incomes, gained access to some level of health care and education, and the relevant statistics for literacy, infant mortality, and life expectancy showed steady improvements. Second, the upper-income groups increasingly sought quality medical care and education in the private sector, often abroad, and lost interest in public education and public health. Trying to meet their obligations, the ministries of health and education eventually became the most impoverished units of the state bureaucracy, and their workers the most poorly paid. Hospitals, secondary schools, and universities that before World War II were the pride of several nations in the region experienced difficulties in managing increased demands and suffered deterioration in many countries.[11] In terms of job protection, the state recognized early that it could not afford unemployment insurance and transferred this obligation to the private sector. Laws made it very difficult or expensive for companies to dismiss workers, hampering them from adjusting the size of their workforces to business cycles, technological improvements, or competition, which had a dampening effect on employment generation. The informal economy, that is, small enterprises operating independent of state regulation and taxation, became the main source of new employment.

To his credit, Prebisch warned of the economic pitfalls in the ISI model. Nonetheless, all relevant actors accustomed themselves to the modus operandi — whose features were high relative prices for domestically produced goods and continued dependence on foreign capital and on commodity exports to finance imports. The economic fallout by the late 1960s included inflation, excessive foreign borrowing, low investment, balance of payments gaps, stagnation of food production, and increasing unemployment. The state's resources for social programs consistently declined on a per capita basis, and state legitimacy declined even in the face of increased appeals to nationalism.

Claims about the "exhaustion" of the ISI model had been extant in the region since the 1970s, but inertia and lack of an alternative preserved ISI well beyond its point of intellectual and practical obsolescence. In every country, those groups favored by the operation of even a flawed development strategy resisted change. Mexico delayed the final day of reckoning by discovering large oil reserves, and all of the countries borrowed extensively abroad in the late 1970s and early 1980s to fund balance of payments deficits. The 1982 debt crisis sounded the death knell for the old model, as Latin America could neither service its debt nor borrow more, and economic, social, and political adjustments ensued.

THE POLITICAL REGIME

The political regime of the statist-national-popular SPM was based on the so-called "compromise state," typically represented by different types of populism independent of regime type. Different authors have utilized this concept to refer to the situation in which, rather than the hegemony of a particular social sector existing in the interior of the state, as in the oligarchic era, there were unstable accommodations among various sectors. Those retaining asymmetric access included diverse factions of the bourgeoisie, middle strata, and industrial workers.[12] Democratic institutions and practices acquired different meanings, according to the political constellations of the times.[13]

In the first Latin American countries to industrialize — Mexico, Brazil, Chile, and Argentina — democratic practices and arrangements were in permanent tension with authoritarian or semi-authoritarian practices. As such, the resulting political formula was a hybrid of democracy and authoritarianism, around which emerged, in an uneven, often implicit, and sometimes tension-ridden fashion, an informal coalition of the most significant social and political actors in order to sustain it.

Political democracy during this historical matrix acquired certain connotations distinct from many of the paradigmatic initial democratizing countries. The Latin American political itinerary differed from that followed by capitalist countries during early industrialization in Western Europe and North America. Democratization in Europe emerged at the end of a long process of gradual evolution, during which many political institutions were preserved from the previous era dominated by the aristocracy.

In contrast, the eclipse of the oligarchic regimes in Latin America in the late 1800s and early 1900s was more rapid in most cases, practically constituting a collapse. The pace of change not only overwhelmed the oligarchy's experiment with restricted democracy, but also seriously eroded its faith in principles associated with liberalism, such as gradualism, checks and balances, and a concern about limiting the power of the state. The oligarchs' loss of political standing did nothing to assuage their suspicions of democracy, while democracy or calls for democracy seemed to them to have a subversive content, suggesting that democratization had a revolutionary potential to transform society.

During the oligarchic period, some of these countries maintained a relative loyalty to constitutional precepts and the subordination of the military to civilian power, in part because the armed forces were involved in the tasks of establishing or defending their countries' national boundaries. In contrast, beginning with the 1920s, the political order began to break up. A stage began of greater instability, with the replacement of nineteenth-century liberal constitutions and more frequent military interventions in politics, often from lower levels in the chain of command. In some countries, stability rested on principles other than the liberal constitutionalism of the oligarchic era. In Uruguay, a reasonably stable political democracy was established in the first decades of the twentieth century. And in Mexico, after the tumultuous two decades that followed the fall of Porfirio Díaz, a nondemocratic order was established that still provided room for social participation and helped lead to a more plural society.

As industrialization, urbanization, and incorporation of greater sectors of the population increased, so also did the greater centrality of the state and politics in society, through formal organizations and informal mechanisms of control over an emerging civil society. The state promoted industrialization and employed a variety of policy tools to create autarkic Latin American economies. It also became the principal mechanism through which different social actors transformed their identities and negotiated, whether implicitly or explicitly, their respective interests and values. In Chile, Uruguay, and Mexico, the party system (multiparty, two-party, or single party) played a central role in articulating these concerns between the state and social sectors.[14]

The theme of democracy was highly visible both with regard to processes of social modernization and an increase in the centrality of the state. From the 1870s to the 1970s, modernization was perceived as broadly progressive. The dominant idea was that the various social sectors — first the middle classes, then miners and workers, and finally the peasantry and the urban poor — were being incorporated or would eventually be incorporated into the material and symbolic benefits of modernization.

The presence and invocation of democracy meant that it became a permanent option for the region, even if this largely did not lead to a consolidation of a democratic political order.[15] During the oligarchic period, the formal constitutional promises of political equality and a rule of law composed one aspect of different countries' histories, as they integrated into the "civilized world." Yet, exclusion, electoral fraud, and state arbitrariness were equally important, if not necessary, for the processes of national integration and economic expansion that were occurring simultaneously.

During the period of the statist-national-popular SPM, suffrage restrictions were gradually eliminated, popular participation expanded through political parties, unions, and in the streets, and the social gaps between the upper classes and the popular and middle sectors narrowed. Nevertheless, with the partial exceptions of Uruguay and Chile (and Costa Rica, though following a somewhat different historical trajectory), political democracy did not fully take root. Too many of the central actors viewed democracy in purely instrumental terms, rather than being committed to it as a normative goal or as a useful method of governance.

The legitimacy of the state during this period remained fragile, depending in great part on its capacity to distribute rewards and benefits. Consequently, neither authoritarian impositions from above nor the channeling of conflict through representative institutions became stable, and effective mechanisms with wide acceptance among key social actors did not emerge. Indeed, both individual and collective actors tended to favor state decision-making processes that were discretionary rather than institutional. This dominant pattern of statist politicization eroded the strength of representative institutions, even if politically democratic regimes were achieved to a greater or lesser extent in various countries of the region.[16]

THE SOCIOCULTURAL MODEL

The statist-national-popular SPM was linked to a broad cultural referent. It was centered on the notion of a popularly based national project and a vision of radical global social change that filled political action with revolutionary overtones. In turn, this project and vision were associated with a type of social action that could be characterized as a central Social Movement. This national-popular Social Movement defined a central conflict and was oriented toward a global social change. Individual historical social movements, despite their particular features, were a part of this overarching SM and, thus, were simultaneously modernizing, developmentalist, national, and oriented toward systemic change, while making reference to "the people" (*el pueblo*) as the only valid historical subject. The emblematic social movement of the statist-national-popular sociopolitical matrix was initially that of the workers' movement, more due to its symbolic importance than to its structural power. Yet, this leadership was challenged at various times because the compromises urban workers occasionally reached with the state or employers led to questions about their revolutionary credentials. Other movements, centered on peasants, students, religious groups, or radical political parties (especially in the 1960s and frequently under the form of a guerrilla force), sometimes sought to assume the leadership of the central Social Movement.

The major characteristics of this SM, composed of different actors and concrete movements, principally urban based, were twofold. The SM, with some variations depending on the country, was heavily symbolic, calling for global social change as well as responses to particularistic concrete demands. Its other characteristic was its reliance on the state as the interlocutor for satisfying these demands and as the site that needed to be conquered in order to bring about these fundamental transformations. The structural weakness of social classes as a base for social movements was mitigated by their ability to attract support through political and ideological mobilization, which sought to be both broadly integrative and revolutionary. Populism was the preferred form of political and collective action under this sociopolitical matrix, notwithstanding other modalities that were more radical, class based, ideological, or even corporatist.

As these kinds of politicization and statism were occurring, in the context of modernization processes marked by growing industrialization, urbanization, and social integration, middle class cultural orientations remained dominant. The middle classes were the primary support for and beneficiaries of the development model. Almost by definition, modernization rested on rationalistic premises and industrialization and emphasized the value of education, especially public schools, as instruments for social mobility.

Culture reflected or reinforced the prevailing social, political, or economic organization. Culture did not become a separate or autonomous sphere of human activity. The developmentalist state promoted cultural policy that was basically democratizing in its social dimension and educational in content, directed to the middle classes.[17] The state tried to deliver to the mass of population, especially urban sectors and "the people," a type of middle class culture that previously had been the patrimony of the elites. The state attempted to promote this type of culture primarily through its educational apparatus and related efforts of extension and diffusion. Beginning in the 1970s, the Latin American cultural dimension became more ideological, incorporating more referents to *lo popular* (that which is of the people), for example, by drawing on urban folklore and popular crafts. The universities, for example, beyond their tasks of educational or scientific-technological development, were increasingly also converted into arenas for citizen participation and social and political mobilization. Among progressive intellectuals and political militants, Marxism, especially in its structural and Leninist visions, became the predominant ideology.[18]

In sum, the cultural dimensions of the dominant SPM did not acquire their own autonomy, dynamism, or density. The exceptions to this rule were societies that experienced revolutionary ferment, such as Chile beginning in 1970, and those with a long tradition of defending national culture, such as Mexico, or in some cases, the maintenance of a popular religiosity. In general, concerns about gender relations, ethnicity, regional identification, or individual demands associated with greater secularization and modernization did not result in self-directed constituencies of social actors. Rather, they were subordinated to the sociopolitical or economic dimensions of the prevailing sociopolitical matrix.

Chapter Three

THE NEW WORLD CONTEXT

GLOBALIZATION

It is commonly said that the principal phenomenon of the current era is globalization, understood in its economic, political, and cultural dimensions, and the social effects that it brings about.[19] The phenomenon is not simply the interdependence among nations or the multiplicity of contacts among them, but rather, the constitution of a unified global space involving asymmetrical relations among its components. Globalization does not necessarily signify homogenization of cultures or the disappearance of patterns of domination and exclusion, but it does bring about their redefinition. Nor is globalization self-regulating.

If economic globalization signifies creation of a global market, a globally integrated production system, and a more unified financial sphere, political globalization has not implied a world government. While domineering geopolitical blocs have disappeared, nation-states are still very much alive. Globalization in the cultural sphere signifies the conversion of a territorial space into a communications space. Globally, we are evolving from a geopolitical world to one that is also geoeconomic and increasingly geocultural. The world that used to divide itself almost exclusively geopolitically — that is, by means of military control over a territorial space — has evolved into one that also defines space and power in communicational and not just territorial space. The models of appropriating communicational space are models of creativity, innovation, knowledge, and subjectivity. Those who propose models of modernity capable of simultaneously combining scientific and technological rationality, subjectivity, affectivity, and historical memory will compete for cultural space in the twenty-first century. Those societies that do not succeed in combining these elements will be less compelling geocultural models.

Latin America had been marked by its double insertion in the geopolitical and geoeconomic worlds. The East-West axis was political and ideological, whereas the North-South axis was economic. With the disappearance of the struggle between the capitalist and communist blocs for world hegemony, the struggles for equality and liberty in the developing world lost their historical-ideological referent. At the same time, the redefinition of the world economic space forced a revision of the twentieth-century development model, based on a mobilized and interventionist state, giving way to the transnational market as

21

the principal axis. All this has resulted in a disarticulation of the traditional relations between the state and society and has transformed the structural bases and representational forms that give rise to social action.

The current phenomenon of globalization, distinguished by an apparent capitalistic homogenization (even in the former Eastern Bloc), has uncovered the new nature of social conflict, characterized by the geopolitical hegemony of the United States, the predominance of neoliberal ideology and policies, and the massive exclusion of vast sectors of the world. Intermixed with the classic forms of struggle from the previous period of worker-peasant-owner confrontation or citizen-state conflict are explosions of identities and particularistic interests, as well as challenges to the norms associated with industrial society. The unifying logic between a single particular strategy of modernization (via industrialization) and a single definition of modernity (industrial society) has been broken, and alternative models of modernity have emerged as legitimate.

THE GLOBAL ECONOMY

What is distinctive about the new economic international context is that we are referring to an era of "global economy" or "global capitalism." From this particular perspective, economic globalization is qualitatively different from the related term, internationalization, even if both sets of processes continue to coexist. While "internationalization" refers simply to the geographical spread of economic activities across national boundaries, "globalization" is a much more complex process that implies increased functional integration among these internationally dispersed activities.[20]

Authors have identified at least six characteristics of the global economy: 1) intensified global competition and the emergence of new centers of production (for example, the NICs); 2) the proliferation, spread, and restructuring of transnational corporations (TNCs); 3) the rapidly advancing technological environment, especially new transportation and communication technologies; 4) a global financial system; 5) the international political environment, including the hegemony of the United States, the economic policies of nation-state, supranational forms of regional economic integration, such as the European Union (EU), the North American Free Trade Agreement (NAFTA), and the Southern Common Market (Mercado Común del Sur — MERCOSUR); and 6) growing global inequalities, both across world regions and inside countries.[21] The first three characteristics are especially evident in changes in the global manufacturing system.

Global Manufacturing

Contemporary industrialization is marked by an integrated system of global trade and production, with dynamic shifts in the geographic location of increasingly fragmented manufacturing processes. These shifts often ignore national boundaries, generating complex regional consequences. Open international trade has encouraged nations to specialize in different branches of manufacturing and even in different stages of production within a specific industry. This process, fueled by the explosion of new products and new technologies since World War II, has led to the emergence of a "global manufacturing system," in which production capacity is dispersed to an unprecedented number of developing as well as industrialized countries.[22] What is novel about today's global manufacturing system is not the spread of economic activities across national boundaries per se, but that international production and trade are globally organized by core corporations that represent both industrial and commercial capital.

Three specific trends in the international economy serve to illustrate the nature of the contemporary global manufacturing system: the spread of diversified industrialization to large segments of the Third World; the shift toward export-oriented development strategies in peripheral nations, with an emphasis on manufactured exports; and high levels of product specialization in the export profiles of most Third World countries, along with continual industrial upgrading by established exporters among the NICs.

Industrial and commercial capital have promoted globalization by establishing two distinct types of international economic networks, which may be called "producer-driven" and "buyer-driven" commodity chains.[23] Producer-driven commodity chains refer to those industries in which TNCs or other large integrated industrial enterprises play the central role in controlling the production system, including its backward and forward linkages. This is most characteristic of capital- and technology-intensive industries such as automobiles, computers, aircraft, and heavy machinery. What distinguishes producer-driven systems is the control exercised by the administrative headquarters of TNCs.

Buyer-driven commodity chains refer to those industries in which large retailers, designers, and trading companies play the pivotal role in setting up decentralized production networks in a variety of exporting countries, typically located in the Third World. This pattern of trade-led industrialization has become common in labor-intensive, consumer goods industries such as garments, footwear, toys, housewares, and consumer electronics. Production is generally carried out by tiered networks of Third World contractors that make finished goods for foreign buyers. Large retailers or designers that order the goods (such as Wal-Mart, J.C. Penney, Nike, or Reebok) supply the specifications; typically, then, though these firms design and/or market, they do not make the branded products they order.

Profitability is greatest in the relatively concentrated segments of the global commodity chains characterized by high barriers to the entry of new firms. Thus, producer-driven commodity chains tend to be controlled by industrial firms at the point of production, whereas retailers and brand-name merchandisers at the marketing and retail end of the chain exercise the main leverage in buyer-driven industries.

Although these processes of change have incorporated most nations into the global manufacturing system, their roles and resources are quite different. Each Third World region is characterized by an internal division of labor involving countries at distinct levels of relative development and with unique patterns of cooperation and competition to exploit this regional potential. After 1930, Latin America invested in industrialization but tended to avoid over-engagement with the international marketplace; its growth rate was much slower and in many years negative. The fact that import substitution industrialization prevailed in Latin America is associated with the presence of producer-driven commodity chains. TNCs that initially focused on the continent's oil, mineral, and agricultural resources gradually shifted to the establishment of more advanced manufacturing industries. In the decades following World War II, ISI factories could be found throughout the region in such sectors as automobiles, machinery, petrochemicals, and pharmaceuticals, with output destined primarily for the domestic market. Beginning in the 1970s, though, in an effort to offset the increasingly costly import bills associated with ISI deepening, some attention was paid to manufactured exports. Yet, buyer-driven commodity chains were practically absent from Latin America, as the TNCs established there were primarily interested in the region's domestic markets. In contrast, the fastest growing Asia-based NICs after 1970 aggressively sought a place in the global manufacturing system, channeled high savings into industry, stressed exports in niche markets, and penetrated international markets initially through buyer-driven commodity chains. Thus, these countries initially gained the overwhelming share of markets in the United States and Europe for profitable consumer goods exports provided by buyer-driven chains.[24]

At the same time, industrialization is no longer necessarily the defining element of national development, as it once was. Industrialization and development are not synonymous, and industrial growth can have quite disparate economic and social consequences, as evident in comparisons of East Asia and Latin America. Furthermore, while industrialization may be a necessary condition for core status in the world system, it is no longer sufficient as the only condition. Continued innovations by the most developed countries tend to make core status an ever-receding frontier, based on a mix of economic activities that require skilled workers, rising wages, and higher levels of value added. By "value added," we mean a mix of economic activities that require skilled workers, rising wages, and more complex technology that enhance the value added to the original components and materials by production processes.

Since the 1950s, the gap between developed and developing countries has been narrowing in terms of industrialization, a trend more clearly present in East and Southeast Asia than in Latin America. As a consequence, industry outstripped agriculture as a source of economic growth in all regions of the Third World. Throughout the developing world, industry as a share of gross domestic product (GDP) has increased over the past several decades, though it showed a slight decline over the 1990s. Agriculture's share has tended to fall, although these changes have been more modest in Latin America than elsewhere, in part due to a relatively high level of manufacturing development by the mid-1960s, earlier than some other regions. In 1990, industry value added in Latin America equaled 36 percent of GDP, declining to 30 percent by 1999; this compares to 40 percent in East Asia and the Pacific in 1990, which rose to 45 percent by 1999, and to 27 percent in 1990 in South Asia, declining slightly to 26 percent in 1999.[25] In the early 1990s, some emerging countries in Asia actually had manufacturing to GDP ratios higher than those for high-income, advanced industrial economies, including Japan.[26] And, in the first decade of this new millennium, it still remains true that the most "developed" nations in the world are no longer the most industrial ones. As core economies shift predominantly toward services, vigorous industrialization has become the hallmark of at least certain parts of the periphery.

In this sense, the regional groupings of less-developed countries — Western Hemisphere, including Latin America and the Caribbean; China; India and the rest of Asia; and sub-Saharan Africa — have sharply contrasting growth profiles. Between 1984 and 1993, Latin America and the Caribbean had extremely low real GDP growth rates, with an annual average of only 2.9 percent, which was estimated to decrease to 2.5 percent over 1994 to 2003. In contrast, China, India, and the rest of developing Asia increased their GDP growth rates over 1984-1993 by an annual average of 10.5 percent, 5.2 percent, and 5.5 percent, respectively. Over the 1994-2003 period, in turn, the annual averages for China, India, and the rest of developing Asia are estimated to be 8.6 percent, 5.9 percent, and 4.0 percent, respectively. Sub-Saharan Africa's GDP grew at an even more modest rate than that of Latin America and the Caribbean over the earlier 1984-1993 period, at an annual average of 1.9 percent, but was projected over the 1994-2003 period to grow at 3.4 percent.[27]

World trade expanded nearly 30-fold in the three decades after 1960. Manufactured goods as a percentage of total world exports increased from 55 percent in 1980 to 75 percent in 1990. Furthermore, the share of the manufactured exports of the NICs that can be classified as "high tech" soared from 2 percent in 1964 to 25 percent in 1985, and those embodying "medium" levels of technological sophistication rose from 16 percent to 22 percent during this same period. This expansion in the quantity and quality of the Third World's export capacity, particularly for manufactured goods, embraces such a diverse array of countries that it appears to be part of a general restructuring in the world

economy. However, these trends were clearly driven primarily by the experience of the Asian economies, whose exports over the 1980s and early 1990s
grew at annual average rates of around 11 percent. In contrast, in Latin America
and the Caribbean, exports were nearly stagnant during the 1970s, with an
annual average growth rate of 0.9 percent, and between 1980 and 1993 grew at
an average annual rate of 3.4 percent.[28]

In exports as in production, manufactures are the chief source of the Third
World's dynamism. The Latin American and Caribbean region, however, has
been a relative laggard in manufacturing exports with differing experiences
across countries and regions. Latin America's main exports have been raw
material supplies, including processed "industrial commodities" and nontraditional agricultural exports, which still make up 80 percent or more of total
exports; the export-oriented assembly of manufactured goods, such as apparel
and electronics items, using imported components; and the manufacture of
advanced industrial products, such as automobiles and computers, within the
integrated production and trade networks of TNCs. Indeed, Latin America's
development hierarchy is evident in the divergent export profiles of individual
countries. Central American and Caribbean nations mainly export agricultural
goods and apparel. The Andean countries are almost exclusively primary-
product exporters, with the exception of Colombia, where manufactured
exports make up one-third of legal exports. Southern Cone countries such as
Argentina and Chile also emphasize primary products, but they have somewhat
higher levels of manufactured exports than are found in the Andean subregion.
Finally, in the region's two largest economies, Brazil and Mexico, manufactured goods account for more than half of total exports; indeed, in the case of
Mexico, as total exports expanded from US$29.2 billion in 1990 to US$124.7
billion in 1998, petroleum declined from representing 35.2 percent of exports
in 1990 to 5.9 percent in 1998, as the value of exports in automobiles, electrical
machinery and appliances, and telecommunications expanded.

Crucial elements of these ties to the global economy and the types of
export roles that countries have are associated with dramatic changes in the
global technological environment and how countries adapt and respond to them.
Technology has had paradoxical effects, distancing wealthier from poorer
countries while seemingly "shrinking" the globe. Over the past decade, the
global technological environment has become exceptionally volatile and inno-
vative. One indicator is that the length of the cycle from innovation to
obsolescence has become shorter; another is that in fields such as biotechnology, basic research is increasingly concentrated in a small number of large
private firms.[29] Because of its dependence on research — a form of national
saving — technology is one element that has extended the distance between rich
and poor countries and dislocated the relations between different sectors inside
each country. Technology has also been an important globalizing influence, as
major transportation and communications breakthroughs have been shrinking

space and time (supertankers, jet aircraft, fax machines, electronic mail, and so on). But technological innovation has not been a strong suit for Latin America. While the region's scientists and technicians have been occasional inventors and innovators in such fields as medicine, mining, and agriculture, these creations generally have related to local products and conditions and have had limited diffusion. Under ISI, Latin America was an importer of frequently outdated technology, employed to produce goods for the local market.

The new technology and communications age is spreading rapidly throughout the region, abetted by deregulation and privatization. This is especially evident in computers and voice and data transmission. The issue is whether Latin American creativity (which certainly helps set world standards in culture, the arts, and literature) can articulate and assert itself through new structures and commercial incentives in science, industry, and medicine and capture an adequate share of the region's savings. In other words, can the region's development model be structured to begin to export patents rather than just pay royalties? To date, this has largely not been the case, which represents one of the many challenges for the region as it shifts toward a new, as yet unconsolidated sociopolitical matrix.

Global Finance

The notion of a global factory incorporates three key changing characteristics: global competition and the emergence of new centers of production; renewed strength and roles for TNCs; and a dramatically evolving technological environment. We can also speak of a "global bank" with separate divisions for savings and deposits, commercial credit, high-net-worth investors, financial intermediation, corporate finance, and equities and securities.[30] The driving forces behind the global bank have been the cost of capital and interest rates, and these have been set, in turn, by investor perceptions of risk/reward and decisions of treasury and central bank officials in rich countries. Unlike a domestic bank, which operates under the supervision of national regulatory authorities, the global bank, particularly as it affects the Third World, has been supervised by international monetary agencies such as the International Monetary Fund (IMF), the World Bank, and the Bank of International Settlements. As in the case of domestic regulators, however, private capital flows and the decisions of investors and money managers are capable of overwhelming the directives of official agencies, making international financial markets increasingly resemble a free-for-all. The significance of the global bank is evident in the fact that all recent economic crises in Latin America have been precipitated not by failures in the production system, but rather in the nexus between domestic and international finance.

In the 1950s, large domestic corporations in rich countries extended their presence throughout the world and consequently became known as TNCs. By the 1960s and 1970s, commercial banks followed the TNCs into their major overseas markets in Europe, Latin America, and Asia. The Eurodollar money supply grew consistently from U.S. trade deficits and bold international investments. The United States' abandonment of the gold standard in 1974 was a clear indicator that markets, not governments, governed international finance, and Eurodollars became the default currency for settling international transactions. The major source of international capital transfers in the Third World initially was foreign direct investment (FDI), followed by foreign grants and assistance, loans from multilateral agencies such as the World Bank, and then in the late 1970s and early 1980s, commercial bank loans.[31]

The debt crisis beginning in 1982 had its origins in the massive exchange of liquidity between oil importing and oil exporting countries in 1974. After the Organization of Petroleum Exporting Countries (OPEC) cartel shocked the world with dramatic price increases in 1974, liquid oil continued to flow east and north. Liquid cash, in turn, was then deposited in New York and London banks, where it was recirculated to many Third World countries in the form of balance of payments loans. The funds transfers ended, however, when petroleum producing countries in the Middle East started drawing down their deposits to finance public works and social projects at home, and historically high inflation in the industrialized world prompted a rise in interest rates. Liquidity dried up, and loans were called, leading to defaults in those countries that had borrowed heavily, particularly in Latin America.[32]

The successful Asian export economies were less affected by the debt crisis. Rather than commercial bank loans, they had based their growth on high savings rates, typically above 30 percent of GDP, which included almost 100 percent retained earnings rates in corporations. Profits plowed back into businesses helped finance international expansion and create a cushion for downturns. Capital flight was minimal. Their commercial bank debt was manageable, and their growth continued apace during the 1980s, when Latin America stagnated and retracted. The Asian model was able to conceal other defects, such as a weakening banking system and speculative investment in real estate.

During the 1970s and 1980s, capital flight out of Latin America was extensive. Indeed, the global bank's divisions for high net worth individuals was extremely busy in Latin America, helping elites to place their dollar deposits in the same London, New York, and Miami branches whose commercial lending divisions suffered huge losses on their Latin American portfolios. By some accounts, the size of these private deposits almost equaled the total commercial bank debt of the Latin American economies. By the rules of accounting, however, the banks absorbed the losses in their own stock equity.

Large banks, including those in Tokyo, simultaneously suffering reversals in their real estate portfolios, needed silent but well coordinated measures from their own regulatory authorities to remain solvent and not shake public confidence in the "global bank."

By the end of the 1980s, Latin American economies could no longer count on the "old" sources of financing. Governmental transfers from rich countries ceased when fiscal restraints forced them to limit investments. Lacking new capital from Organization for Economic Cooperation and Development (OECD) countries, the multilateral agencies could not increase credits. Multinationals saw greater opportunities in Asia, particularly China. Commercial bankers who suffered through the debt crisis were not about to propose new unsecured loans. At the same time, Latin America was capital starved, and rich countries still had capital to export.

In the 1990s, private capital flows to Latin America returned,[33] in part, because of significant measures of financial liberalization within the region. Privatization of state industries, utilities, and banks encouraged capital to enter primarily as FDI and as portfolio investments (stocks, securities, bonds, and other monetary instruments).[34] These reforms, however, also made it relatively easy for capital to depart, increasing the vulnerability of Latin American markets and their economies to foreign shocks — as happened in Mexico in 1995, the "Tequila effect"; in Mexico, Argentina, and to a lesser extent Brazil and Chile in 1997, the "Asian flu"; and again in Brazil in 1999, the "Baixa Nova." And, Argentina's so-called *corralito* (little corral), in late 2001, was an attempt to protect besieged branches of mainly foreign-owned banks from massive withdrawals of dollars and pesos by anxious and angry middle-class depositors.

As with industrial processes, in finance there has been a dramatic increase in the integration of what were once more dispersed international activities, together with a weakening of national institutions' ability to run, control, or even regulate them. Global financial markets are based on market predominance over regulatory bodies, increased information flow, rapid movement of capital, and an almost instantaneous "stampede to quality" in times of trouble. Traders in London, Tokyo, New York, and Chicago help fix the value of currencies, the level of foreign reserves, and long-term interest rates. A multitude of computer-based technologies combined with television and satellite business news services with global reach disseminate relevant market news to investors and consumers with very little lag time. Portfolio investments in securities, short-term deposits, and secondary markets for bonds seek markets where funds can enter and exit quickly. Portfolio managers' bonuses are based partly on their ability to pull funds at the first sign of a potential downturn. National investors in domestic economies often precipitate the crisis, through a run on dollar reserves after losing faith in their political and financial leadership. Such was the case after political assassinations and indigenous insurrection in Mexico, legislative stalemates in Ecuador and Brazil, and a foreign debt moratorium in Argentina. And, during electoral campaigns, the growth in interest rate spreads between national bond instruments and U.S. Treasury bonds can be focused on as an indicator of the "political risk" that international markets perceive in an opposition candidate, thus seeking to discredit him, as was the ultimately unsuccessful case with Luiz Inácio Lula da Silva in his successful presidential race in Brazil in 2002.

The painful lessons of the 1980s have induced institutional investors to act as financial intermediaries by selling assets immediately and "getting them off the books." The shifting of risk to transient and opportunistic investors seeking an adequate reward/risk ratio means that national economies have few long-term friends in major financial institutions. When times are good, investment banks flood in to bid for business at high fees, deliver capital, distribute securities to their investor network, and depart hurriedly in search of the next deal. When a company or economy hits a bump in the road, these same banks are unavailable to provide emergency assistance but will intermediate a rescue facility at higher rates and higher fees. The investment banking business is not without risks, however, as a drop in currency values or a shift in interest rates can upset programmed hedge instruments, resulting in large losses for First World investment banks with highly leveraged positions. This occurred mainly with Spanish banks operating in Argentina in the 2001-2002 crisis.

The exigencies of the global bank obliged many Latin American economies to adopt new internal processes. Privatization of state enterprises was to be a mechanism to balance the government budget and create assets that attracted international capital. Dollarization would help project an image of financial maturity as well as push inflation down to world averages. Fiscal reforms — such as balanced budgets, tax enforcement, and pension reform — were to help increase the domestic savings rate. Robust short-term capital markets, including time deposits in dollars, were to help attract portfolio investment and maintain a positive balance of payments. Stock markets would provide another means of attracting domestic and international capital. And, investment deregulation could induce large multinationals to favor capital expenditures in Latin America over Asia, Europe, or Africa.

Thus, for many countries in Latin America, the situation at the end of the twentieth century was considerably different from the early 1980s, when state enterprises were sacrosanct, foreign exchange was officially regulated, inflation was tolerated and even encouraged, capital markets were primitive, and stock markets were ridiculed. Yet, many of the reforms that were implanted neglected, distorted, or exploited the socio-historical context, and the changes in most countries have not yet been translated into sustained foreign investment flows or economic growth rates. Privatizations were riddled by corruption, and frequently new owners did not abide by contractual re-investment agreements. Convertibility in Argentina, unaccompanied by fiscal and other reforms, ultimately bankrupted the economy. Domestic stock markets continued to be manipulated and more volatile than in the more developed countries. As Latin America entered the twenty-first century, the combined effects were disinvestments in the region after an initial surge and markets that regained a reputation for being highly risky. At the same time, it is clear that powerful international forces helped to restructure economic practices in Latin America and undermine the old statist-national-popular sociopolitical matrix.

OTHER FORMS OF GLOBALIZATION

Economic globalization has precedents in Latin America in the nineteenth century, when the region received large European and U.S. investments and its economies were export oriented. Even in the sixteenth and seventeenth centuries, the region formed part of a world economic system and was largely responsible for the relative prosperity of its colonial patrons, Spain and Portugal, which were world powers at the time. The main differences in the twentieth and twenty-first centuries are the velocity of communications and the ease of physical mobility of persons, which support the economic transformations but also affect culture, identities, and social movements.[35]

Popular movies and youth-oriented music from North American and European countries dominate cinemas and urban radio stations throughout Latin America, introducing their audiences to a phenomenon sometimes called cultural imperialism. Lack of financing plays a large part in the dearth of domestically produced alternatives, but the fact is that Latin American audiences choose to go to foreign movies and listen to stations formatting imported music in preference to local production. TV programming contains considerable Latin American content, and the most popular *telenovelas* from Mexico, Brazil, and Venezuela have audiences in the United States, Western Europe, and Russia, and not just among immigrants from Latin America. The popularity of many musical styles and artists in the North that have Latin American roots demonstrates that globalization in the cultural field is a two-way street.

Communications also play a role in elevating the saliency of public policy issues. An example is the environmental movement, which began in Europe and the United States and was initially widely resisted in Latin America. Business, government, opinion leaders, and even average citizens believed that an insistence on environmental protection was a subterfuge to slow down Latin American economic growth and maintain a situation of dependency. Such opposition did not prevent foreign foundations from financing nascent environmental civil society organizations or large northern non-governmental organizations (NGOs) from establishing chapters in Latin American countries. Nor did it block the coverage of environmental issues via Cable News Network

(CNN) broadcasts, British Broadcasting Corporation (BBC) programming in Spanish, and news reports of citizens' and judicial actions against polluters in industrialized countries.

Awareness of the environmental devastation in noncapitalist Eastern Europe helped undermine simplistic dependency arguments. At the same time, investigative reporting by domestic news media (including *O Globo*, *La Nación*, El Universo, and Televisa) of profit-taking from forests, rivers, oceans, and mining areas by investors with virtually no concern for the public good helped create a new attitude among citizens toward the environment, intensified by the high levels of smog in cities like Mexico City, São Paulo, and Santiago. At least some major Latin American companies discovered that it was to their advantage to improve their environmental records through best practices embodied in the International Organization for Standardization's standards, such as ISO 9003, not only for their public image but also to improve their competitiveness in the world economy. Many of their manufacturing and distribution customers in industrialized countries gave them a period of time to certify that their products were manufactured with environmental safeguards before cutting off orders. Surveys showed that even Latin American consumers considered environmental responsibility to be a criterion in purchasing decisions. Yet, progress on critical environmental issues remains slow and uncertain.

Non-state terrorism (that is, violent political acts perpetrated by system opponents against random civilians) has been infrequent in Latin America and locally concentrated.[36] In the late twentieth century, the most prominent cases have been acts by criminal elements, such as the narcotics mafia in Colombia seeking to influence government policy or to prevent extradition, and by some guerrilla movements, such as Sendero Luminoso (Shining Path) in Peru, demoralizing the public and de-legitimizing the government. To be sure, in the 1970s and 1980s, one of the most notorious international terrorists (Ilich Ramírez Sánchez aka Carlos the Jackal) involved in airplane hijackings and bombings was born in Venezuela, but the region has not been a platform or locus for international terrorism.[37]

The region could not forever insulate itself from terrorism as a weapon used to confront political issues in other parts of the world. The relative ease of personal mobility and communication (fax, encrypted e-mail) facilitated this transformation. In 1992, international terrorists arranged the bombing of the Israeli Embassy in Buenos Aires, followed two years later by the bombing of the Israeli Mutual Association of Argentina (Asociación Mutual Israelita de Argentina — AMIA). Foreign agents paid Argentine collaborators to carry out these acts of violence. Soon after the September 11, 2001, attacks on New York and Washington, officials announced the existence of a Middle Eastern terrorist cell in the permeable Argentina-Paraguay-Brazil border near Iguaçu Falls, and several Latin American countries arrested suspected terrorists in their midst. Communications created instantaneous and almost universal awareness of the September attack, which made informed Latin Americans as anxious about their personal safety as citizens in northern countries. Generalized uncertainty had a dampening effect on the Latin American economies, particularly those most intertwined with the United States.

The global reach of terrorism has had both psychological and economic consequences for Latin America. One country that experienced a dramatic decline in attention from the United States was Mexico. President Vicente Fox of Mexico had been the first foreign head of state to visit with President George W. Bush after his inauguration, and the Fox administration had initially expected that significant advances with regard to a more rational immigration policy were possible in the short term. Yet, the new security concerns of the United States soon placed this issue on the back burner. Another country that felt the shift in U.S. policy was Colombia. The political violence in Colombia has overwhelmingly affected civilian noncombatants, particularly through actions carried out by the paramilitary groups organized under the umbrella of the United Self-Defense Forces of Colombia (Auto Defensas Unidas de Colombia — AUC), though also by the Revolutionary Armed Forces of Colombia (Fuerzas Armadas Revolucionarias de Colombia — FARC), and by the smaller Army of National Liberation (Ejército de Liberación Nacional — ELN). Yet, until the attacks of September 2001, the extensive expansion in U.S. military aid for Colombia was officially linked with counternarcotics purposes, though in practice it had also been targeted for counterinsurgency. Following the attacks, the flow of U.S. military assistance to Colombia initially declined from the heights it had reached under the Clinton administration, as did attention to drug trafficking in general, due to the shift in attention toward the Al Qaeda (The Base) network, associated countries, and security threats within the United States. Yet, over 2002, as the political violence in Colombia was increasingly viewed as a terrorist problem, and especially following the inauguration of Alvaro Uribe as the new president of Colombia, military assistance flows from the United States to Colombia once again increased.

What the most important consequences of the September attacks would be for the region were uncertain early in 2003. One might be the rediscovery of the importance and value of a coherent, functioning state by the United States, though whether this would extend beyond functions of national defense and domestic security, now focused on the threat of terrorism rather than communism, remained unclear. Another consequence, though, might be the relative marginalization of Latin America and of issues central to the region — such as finance, trade, and migration — from United States' concerns.

THE INTERNATIONAL ENVIRONMENT AND
THE ROLE OF STATE POLICIES

The global economy implies an international political environment that incorporates supranational forms of regional economic integration, in spite of the fits and starts through which they have emerged and develop, as well as the economic policies of nation-states. At two levels, state policies are important for new export roles that are emerging through global commodity chains: the protectionist policies of governments in advanced industrial countries and the development strategies of Third World nations. State policies at these two levels are interactive, as the success of Third World efforts to promote export-oriented industrialization stimulated protectionism in developed countries.

Protectionism is evident for manufactured goods but particularly for agricultural goods. Exports of manufactured goods, including food products, from Third World countries to the advanced industrial countries face tariffs that, on average, are four times higher than those facing exports by industrial countries to the same market; furthermore, these tariffs also typically escalate, based on the level of processing. Yet, protectionist policies are even more evident with regard to agricultural products, through such measures as tariffs, quotas, and export subsidies. Tariffs imposed by industrial countries on agricultural products such as meat, sugar, and dairy products from less-developed countries are almost five times higher than those on manufactured products. As a consequence, while global trade in manufactured goods grew by 5.8 percent per year from 1985 to 1994, global trade in agricultural goods grew at only 1.8 percent per year during this period.[38]

At the same time, these protectionist policies in the core countries have played a major role in fostering the observed pattern of globalization of economic activity. Tariffs, import quotas, and other protectionist measures have been used by the European Community (EC), the United States, and Canada since the 1960s to regulate trade in industries such as textiles and apparel, footwear, automobiles, color televisions, and appliances.[39] Particular attention was focused on manufactured exports from Japan and the East Asian NICs. Although the original intent of these policies was to protect developed country firms from a flood of low-cost imports that threatened to disrupt major domestic industries, the result was exactly the opposite: protectionism heightened the competitive capabilities of Third World manufacturers.[40] However, the fact that during this period Latin American countries de-emphasized exports as a national economic goal limited their ability to develop competitive industries.

Industrial upgrading in the NICs was one of the major consequences of import quotas because it permitted successful Asian exporters to maximize foreign exchange earnings and profitability of quantitative restrictions on trade. Japan had followed a similar strategy in the automobile industry. Protectionism by core countries has had a second consequence as well: the diversification of foreign competition. The imposition of quotas on an ever widening circle of Third World exporters has led producers in Japan and the East Asian NICs, who also have had to contend with escalating labor costs and currency appreciation, to open up new satellite factories in low-wage overseas countries that offer either a quota advantage or a labor advantage.

An important affinity exists between the ISI and EOI (export-oriented industrialization) strategies of national development and the structure of commodity chains, as noted in an earlier section. Import substitution occurs in the same kinds of capital- and technology-intensive industries represented by producer-driven commodity chains (such as steel, aluminum, petrochemicals, machinery, automobiles, and computers). In addition, the main economic agents in both cases are TNCs and state-owned enterprises. Export-oriented industrialization, in contrast, is usually channeled through buyer-driven commodity chains, where production in labor-intensive industries is concentrated in small to medium-sized private domestic firms located mainly in the Third World. Historically, the export-oriented development strategy of the East Asian NICs and buyer-driven commodity chains emerged together in the early 1970s, suggesting a close connection between the success of EOI and the development of new forms of organizational integration in buyer-driven industrial networks.

These export-oriented development strategies often lead to the fragmentation rather than integration of national economies, however. ISI policies of the past established a pattern of segmentation by nation-state in which parallel national industries were set up to supply highly protected domestic markets with finished goods, thus reinforcing other aspects of the kind of sociopolitical matrix established at that time. The more recent turn to EOI, often in conjunction with continuing ISI, has fostered a logic of transnational integration, based on geographical specialization and global sourcing. As a result, national economies may become increasingly segmented by region and sector with enclaves maintaining greater links to external corporations than to complementary domestic businesses. Mexico provides an excellent example of a country that has made significant shifts from primary products to manufactured exports and experienced export diversification, yet continues to suffer from significant limitations. Over the past decade, these dynamic economic shifts have not translated into higher real wages for workers, and most Mexican consumers are not better off than they were 10 years ago. In addition, there is a dramatic gap between the number of jobs created and the number of youth entering the job market, even as there is a sharp division between the "Dollar Mexico" linked to the international market and the "Peso Mexico," which makes goods for often poverty-stricken local consumers.[41] These types of gaps, frequently with additional complicating regional, ethnic, and gender dimensions, may be found with national variations throughout the continent.

Thus, state policy has a major impact on global commodity chains and more broadly on development patterns. In EOI, though, governments are primarily facilitators; they are condition-creating and tend not to become directly involved in production. Governments try to generate the infrastructure support needed to make export-oriented industries work. These include modern transportation facilities and communications networks; bonded areas, such as export-processing zones or *maquiladoras* found in Mexico, Central America, and the Caribbean; subsidies for raw materials; customs drawbacks for imported inputs that are used in export production; and adaptive financial institutions and easy credit (for example, facilitating the ability of small firms to obtain letters of credit). In ISI, governments have played a much more interventionist role. They used the full array of industrial policy instruments, such as local content requirements, joint ventures with domestic partners, and export promotion schemes, while the state often became involved in production activities, especially in upstream (supplying) industries, which typically made intermediate products such as steel and petrochemicals.

The role of the state at the point of production tends to be facilitative in buyer-driven commodity chains and more interventionist in producer-driven chains. However, there is an important caveat for buyer-driven chains. Since these are export-oriented industries, state policies in the consuming or importing countries, such as the United States, also are highly significant. This is where the impact of protectionist measures — quotas, tariffs, and voluntary export restraints — imposed by the United States or other major consumer countries shapes the location of production in buyer-driven chains. If one compares the global sourcing of apparel, where quotas are prevalent (currently under the World Trade Organization's (WTO) 10-year transitional program that began in 1995 and is due to remove all quotas by 2005), and footwear, which has no quotas, one sees that far more countries are involved in the production and export networks for clothes than for shoes. This is basically a quota effect, whereby the array of Third World apparel export bases is continually being expanded to bypass the import ceilings mandated by quotas against previously successful apparel exporters. In short, the globalization of export production has been fostered by two distinct sets of state policies: Third World efforts to promote EOI, coupled with protectionism in developed country markets.

Trade agreements and economic integration have formed part of Latin American countries' strategies to generate exports and control volatility in their own markets. The most well-known initiatives in the 1990s and into the new decade have been NAFTA and MERCOSUR. However, these are but two of more than two dozen agreements that are joining countries in never-ending combinations, including many at great geographic distance. NAFTA has joined the United States, Canada, and Mexico in a trade and investment agreement, which has called for the elimination of tariffs and investment restrictions among the countries over a period extending as long as 15 years. MERCOSUR (known in Brazil as MERCOSUL) has joined Brazil, Argentina, Uruguay, and Paraguay, plus Chile and Bolivia as associate members, in an emerging common market, which has stated its intention to eliminate tariffs and investment restrictions gradually among the member countries, as well as to establish a common external tariff for imported foreign goods.[42] These agreements implicitly have favored some domestic and international actors over others, and proponents have not camouflaged the fact that all trade reform measures have "winners and losers." Within Latin American countries, winners have been mainly large industries with the capacity to rationalize costs to compete in the larger market; financial actors with investment capital to permit expansion into economies of other member states; and service providers who have seen barriers to entry drop away in transportation, construction, insurance, accounting, and health.[43] Losers have been peasants, redundant workers, small business owners, small retailers, and certain industries (like small-scale mining) that require subsidies or tax exoneration to keep afloat.

Critics of economic opening are those who believe trade agreements can hobble the movement toward a truly efficient global economy or those who lose their businesses or who take the side of the losers. The first group argues that NAFTA and MERCOSUR are trade and investment diverting (that is, they only redirect product or capital flow, rather than increase them); lock in inefficiencies and cross-subsidies (albeit in larger economic units); and are unfairly biased against nonmembers. The second group of opponents includes those who distrust capitalism as a rationalizing agent because its benefits accrue mainly to economic elites, and globalization's short-term effects for large numbers of people can be impoverishment rather than enrichment. A third group comprises those who are fearful that they will be forced out of business when external competition invades their previously protected markets. They reject the argument that the losers eventually would lose anyway or that accelerating economic rationalization will permit the economy to grow more rapidly and eventually employ displaced workers in new, competitive industrial sectors. All opponents correctly sense that trade agreements or common markets are a sign of a fundamental change in the development model and a departure from the prevailing sociopolitical matrix.

In the Latin American region, proponents of both arguments have found empirical support for their positions. Globalization has improved the international competitiveness of many parts of the region, overall levels of exports have expanded, and at least some industrial upgrading has occurred. In spite of the fact that national industrial policy has been sharply curtailed, local capital is holding its own. Domestic firms are most prominent as producers in nontraditional export activities, assemblers in export processing zones or *maquiladoras*, and component suppliers in the advanced manufacturing sectors. Regional integration schemes such as NAFTA and MERCOSUR create incentives for the regionalization of commodity chains, which create the potential for backward and forward linkages.

However, Latin America's experience with globalization in the 1980s, 1990s, and into the new decade remains highly problematic. Overall, the region's technology-intensive exports to global markets remain very low. Furthermore, high and growing levels of inequality in income distribution limit domestic markets and generate an over-reliance on exports, even as the region is more marked by deep national and regional economic asymmetries. TNCs have reasserted their importance in the region. By the early 1990s, portfolio investment and FDI had replaced international commercial bank loans as the primary source of foreign capital. TNCs are now the dominant force in each of Latin America's three main export roles: resource-based sectors, traditional manufacturing industries, and advanced manufactured goods. In addition, given the neoliberal emphasis on privatization in Latin America, TNCs have fortified their dominant role by recapturing strategic positions in Latin America's extractive and intermediate goods industries, as well as in burgeoning new service sectors like telecommunications and banking.

Over a two decade period, the dominant development model in Latin America's largest countries changed significantly. Abandoning state-owned, self-sufficient industries producing for a domestic market, the model increasingly stressed economic integration, driven by rules of comparative advantage, competitiveness, and the blurring of national-foreign distinctions. Latin America increased its presence in both producer- and buyer-driven commodity chains, for example, Brazilian steel and Mexican *maquiladoras*. Primary production, from petroleum to bananas, still constituted the majority of exports heading north. Yet, there were several significant new trends with contradictory effects. These included the dollarization of domestic financial markets; the emergence of more concentrated power in the hands of domestic economic conglomerates, sometimes associated with foreign investors, through privatization processes which too often were managed in a corrupt manner and led to unregulated private monopolies; the discovery and exploitation of sales opportunities in neighboring countries by Latin American businesses; and the dilution of economic nationalism as a rallying cry for national unity.

HISTORICAL ROUTES OF INTEGRATION INTO THE WORLD ECONOMIC AND POLITICAL SYSTEM

As we reflect on the relationship between the Latin American development model and world trends set by the leading industrialized countries over the past long century, we can identify various historical periods. The first is from 1870 to 1914, when the larger Latin American countries began their integration into the world economy. The second is from 1914 to 1945, when these countries began defining their protectionist alternative in the face of increasing disorganization at the world capitalist level, particularly from the 1930s on, the decade in which the statist-national-popular SPM began emerging in the larger and early modernizing countries in the region (see Chapter Two). The third is from 1945 to the mid-1970s, which clearly marks a bifurcation between dominant world trends and Latin America's more autarkic, developmentalist orientation. During the current contemporary period, the continent has been moving away from bifurcation and returning to earlier affinities regarding the world capitalist system.

In broad terms, from 1870 to 1914, the world economy was marked by a laissez-faire ideology, and the Latin American oligarchy increasingly supported liberal capitalism as an ideology, while nations in the continent were engaged in state building. During this period, Latin American countries tended to follow the dominant world trend of more open economic relations, enjoying substantial export-led growth, growing foreign investment, and stronger states. This was particularly evident in the cases of the larger and other early modernizing countries in the region, such as Mexico, Brazil, and the Southern Cone countries of Argentina, Chile, and Uruguay; only secondarily among the late modernizing Andean countries of Colombia, Peru, and Venezuela, plus Costa Rica in Central America; and barely at all among the remaining late-late modernizing countries, particularly the other Andean countries and most in Central America and the Caribbean.

Outward-oriented growth and integration into the expanding world economy led by Europe provided the material resources and the politico-ideological rhetoric for nation building during the five decades prior to World War I. During this period, the economic architecture of the new Latin American nations was both pro-laissez-faire and dirigiste. On the one hand, market principles were consistently advanced and defended. Thus, free trade in both directions was favored; raw materials and foodstuffs were exported, and manufactured products were imported. The flow of international capital was promoted by Latin American governments in a context in which capital markets performed their task with virtually no official intervention or restriction.[44] And, most countries adhered to the gold standard and tried to defend the convertibility of their currencies. On the other hand, state intervention was often used to cushion export sectors from the adverse effects of overproduction gluts in the world market and the obsolescence of specific commodities or backward production techniques.

Latin America's new nations were among offspring of the expansion of international trade and industrial capitalism. This process accelerated precisely at the time the region was fully integrating into the world economy, during the half century prior to World War I. In fact, one can argue that Latin America "over integrated" into the fin de siècle British-led world economic system.

Unlike the United States or Japan, Latin America was, like czarist Russia, always heavily dependent on foreign investment for capital accumulation. And, unlike the United States and many countries in Europe, which witnessed protectionist reactions to the British-inspired free trade architecture, in Latin America protectionist forces were scarce and feeble.

The subsequent period from 1914 to 1945 was marked by the disorganization of free market capitalism, with an intensification of protectionist strategies in Western Europe and the United States, especially after 1930. Indeed, over the 1930-1945 period, world trade fell sharply, as did the international flow of capital, and economies declined. Key Latin American countries such as Argentina, Brazil, and Chile created larger, more bureaucratized states and protected their internal markets to substitute for the space left by the world economy. Thus, during this period, Latin American trends were still largely consistent with those of the industrialized countries.

World War I irreversibly damaged the informal, albeit integrated, system of capital and European population flows, as well as trade exchanges that were centered on Great Britain. After World War I, the United States became, for all practical purposes, the world's only net creditor. This trend was dramatically reflected in Latin America. While United States' investment in the region had been marginal before 1913, between 1920 and 1931, U.S. new capital issues in the region were US$2 billion against a mere £51 million issued by Great Britain.[45]

The replacement of Great Britain by the United States as the region's primary investor was not only a change of the center but was also associated with major transformations in the economic and political architecture of the world that were to affect Latin America's links to it and to redefine radically the economic and political configuration of the majority of the countries of the region. The breakdown of the pre-war informal order of international capitalism opened a period of more than three decades in which the decline of trade and capital investment was largely an effect of the intensification of international and intra-national conflict.

In the major capitalist countries, the 1914-1945 period — particularly during the Great Depression after 1930 — witnessed a series of concatenated processes. These included 1) the intensification of the autarkic protectionist strategies in Western Europe and North America, 2) the increasingly unsettled relations of European nation states, 3) the politicization of conflicts between labor and capital and subsidiarily between farmers and consumers, and 4) the emergence of alternative political formulae in the transition to rule by popular mandate.[46] After World War I, the capitalist core countries became more autonomous to the extent that international trade decreased and growth became more inward-oriented. At the same time, these countries became more interdependent because each one's economic policies was more interrelated with the others. Moreover, there was a major difference between Western Europe's and

Latin America's early modernizers. International conflicts and the threat of war permanently loomed on the political horizon of European nations, causing them to draw closer together; this perverse but nonetheless effective mechanism of integration was largely absent in Latin America.

The trends prevailing in the 1920s were precursors of what was going to come during the next one and one-half decades. During the Depression and war years, as Carlos Díaz-Alejandro perceptively analyzed, there were two distinct reactions in Latin America to these transformations and the breakdown of the international laissez-faire order. The majority of the Andean, Central American, and Caribbean countries (the late and late-late modernizers) kept trying to enforce the precepts of free market orthodoxy. The attempts to rely on the gold standard and free trade were largely unsuccessful, but this outcome did not lead these countries to implement protectionist policies or other instruments of state interventionism. Rather, most of them resorted to forging closer commercial linkages to the United States and the industrialized European nations to attempt to secure a steady share of their markets.[47]

In turn, the larger countries and/or early modernizers, first hesitantly and then with more determination, embarked on an altogether different route: the abandonment of free market orthodoxy and the promotion of ISI. In a sense, Mexico and the Southern Cone countries replicated on a minor scale the same routes that the majority of the developed North Atlantic economies had followed at least since the end of World War I: unorthodox economic policies, partial disintegration from the international system, and inward-oriented growth. According to Díaz-Alejandro, the strategy of "disintegration from the disintegrating world economy" was clearly more successful than the alternative path of persisting to integrate fully into it. It was also evident, as Díaz-Alejandro suggests, that the de-linking strategy required a degree of national sovereignty that was largely absent in most of the other countries of Latin America.[48]

However, during the subsequent period, roughly from 1945 to the 1970s, a bifurcation emerged. The industrialized countries moved to open their economies and to engage in competitive world commerce. Even if this shift was partial and incomplete, it still stood in sharp contrast with most Latin American countries that retained closed economies wedded to the logic of ISI. Thus, in the decades following World War II, the Latin American development model grew further out of touch with the dominant world trend.

The major outcome of World War II was the emergence of a new international economic and political order. Several decades before 1914, informal international arrangements had been disorganized. After 1945, the political economy of the capitalist system shifted in the direction of institutionalization of rules at the international level and greater uniformity of political formulae at the domestic level. This process involved several major transformations, of which we will briefly highlight five.

First, the United States became a more willing economic and political center of the capitalist world system. The geopolitical and economic competition with the socialist bloc led by the Soviet Union turned into one of the central aspects of U.S. hegemony. Due to the Cold War nuclear stalemate in Europe, semiperipheral regions like Latin America became the sites of more open confrontations between the two superpowers. The region thus gained a geopolitical importance that was, in fact, the reverse of its overall declining importance in the international economic system.

Second, the shape of the vast majority of Western European and North American governments converged into a relatively uniform political formula, combining different variants of competitive party systems and the building of different types of Keynesian welfare states.[49] As a corollary, representative democracy became the key for membership in the club of First World countries.

Third, during the late 1940s and early 1950s the reorganization and renewed dynamism of the world's economy was based upon the reconstruction of capital markets. Funded by the United States, the Marshall Plan and, somewhat later, the International Bank for Reconstruction and Development (IBRD, called The World Bank or The World Bank Group) initially played important roles. Gradually, Western European countries and Japan increased their relevance to the world's economy. The founding of the IMF in 1945 made possible the emergence of a stable monetary system, resting on fixed exchange rates in the largest capitalist economies. And finally, there was a strong and sustained revitalization of world trade within the framework of a liberal multilateral system and the establishment in 1947 of the General Agreement on Tariffs and Trade (GATT).[50]

Fourth, the pre-1939 international economic system had been a mosaic of intensely competitive autarkic units. After the end of the war, the autarkic strategies were not discarded, though they were mitigated. Thus, although mechanisms for stimulating inward-oriented growth were kept and domestic actors, such as industrial manufacturing firms, banks, farmers, and wage earners, were partially insulated from international competition, overall there was clearly a much more liberalized international trade structure.

And, fifth, Latin American countries became increasingly marginal players in the new political economy of the capitalist system. This was clearly reflected in their almost insignificant role in the rebuilt international organizations. The participation of the region in world trade decreased, Latin American countries were excluded from private capital markets, and their currencies were irrelevant within the new international monetary equilibrium.

The perseverance of autarkic strategies and the deepening of ISI in Brazil, Mexico, and the Southern Cone — countries in which the statist-national-popular sociopolitical matrix most clearly emerged — had a demonstration effect in other countries of the region that had persisted in their traditional role of raw material exporters and importers of manufactured products during the interwar years. Beginning in the late 1940s, this was particularly apparent in Colombia, Peru, and Venezuela, where the size of the internal market was comparatively larger than in Central America and the Caribbean. Moreover, during the 1950s, a growing number of U.S. and European transnational manufacturing corporations developed a strategy in Latin America that was different from the one that was unfolding in the countries where their headquarters were located. They began to open plants in the larger Latin American countries in order to circumvent the protectionist barriers created after the Depression, thus channeling their production into the domestic market of each country. This strategy intensified the negative effects that ISI had on the competitiveness and the comparative efficiency of Latin American economies.[51] Finally, as discussed in Chapter Two, buttressing the deepening of ISI and its expansion into additional countries was the emergence of a practical ideology, known as developmentalism (*desarrollismo* in Spanish and *desenvolvimentismo* in Portuguese), that gave it theoretical and political legitimacy.[52]

A renewed process of increasing disorganization of the international economic system began in the 1970s. By the late 1970s, the major Latin American countries were following policies that remained vastly inconsistent with the major world capitalist forces. The Latin American approach appeared less and less viable and began to break down, as countries in the region began a long and painful process of greater reinsertion into the world economy. The perceived need for this reinsertion then became even more acute over the 1990s, as consequences of international political changes following the collapse of the Soviet Union; the perceived lack of viability of the state socialist model; and changes in production, commerce, and finance induced by other globalization processes.

What this means is that Latin America has moved to resemble more closely the contemporary dominant trends in the world economy, as it did in certain prior periods. The persistence of the region's economic policy shortcomings and traumatic social adjustments derive in part from the region's attempt to become realigned with these dominant international patterns, all the while maintaining other incentives and supports also inherited from the past. Whether greater integration with world markets will be a backdrop to a successful model of development and a new SPM (as occurred for some countries in the region during an earlier period with the statist-national-popular SPM) remains to be seen.

Yet, a shift in the development model from autarky to globalization cannot be neutral for a nation's populace, and it is not surprising that it has been identified by terms such as disintegration, displacement, destruction, and decline. The people who have been damaged, at least in the short term, are the majority of those living in the region and include workers in low-paying and low-skill jobs, peasants in subsistence or traditional export sectors, consumers hurt by devaluation and eroding standards of living, and firms unable to compete in increasingly open markets. The beneficiaries include exporters, particularly those who are able to add value to local products; financiers with access to both local and hard currency; investors in "cleaned-up" privatized state industries; skilled workers; junior managers in internationally competitive sectors; and service providers catering to international businesses, such as accountants, lawyers, consultants, trainers, and engineers. While the state's ability to define and defend national economic interests is shrinking, the demands placed on it for social programs to handle those who are marginalized or unable to compete in the global economy are growing.

Thus, in this context, the region now faces the need to construct a new development model in the broad sense, bringing together not only economic but also political, social, and cultural elements. A sociopolitical matrix is not defined by its development model, but a development model does provide the conditions for elective affinities to emerge across components of the SPM and can serve as a legitimizing force. In the next chapter, we focus on how globalization and domestic pressures and factors have interacted to create pressures for change across political, social, and cultural dimensions, in addition to new tensions and as yet unrealized possibilities for the articulation of a new sociopolitical matrix.

Chapter Four

POLITICAL, SOCIAL, AND CULTURAL CHALLENGES

Transformations wrought by the forces of economic globalization are crucial to understanding the current issues faced by the countries in the region. Yet, they are not the only transformations that affect the region, nor are they themselves immune from developments in the political, social, and cultural spheres. The multiplicity of these changes and the causal interconnections among them are a challenge to contemporary social science and its analytical categories. The concept of a sociopolitical matrix helps guide analysis and understanding of these societies in this contemporary period.

As described above, the effects of and the responses to economic globalization have brought pressures within the region for a dramatic change in the model of development, conceived in a specific, economic sense of the term rather than a holistic one.[53] This change pertains to the shift from an "inward oriented" model to the various new forms of insertion into the international economy discussed above, as well as to new relations between the state and society. The previous development model centered on the domestic generation of an industrial society in which social classes became the "allies of development" around a national, proactive, and mobilizing state as the "agent of development."[54] However, under the impact of globalization, the state has tended to lose its hegemonic role as an agent of development. The state shares this role with the market and the private sector, where cadres of business leaders in several countries seek, for the first time since the 1930s, to constitute themselves as a ruling class.

The new emerging global development model turns on transnational market forces as its principal axis, which reduces the scope of action of classic national actors and the capacity for intervention of the national state. The overriding questions of this new context are not simply or ingenuously — how to free up markets or how to carry out privatizations. Rather, the challenges are exactly the opposite: How can the autonomy of national actors and the state be elevated in societies crisscrossed by powerful external influences, and how, in the new polity, can the notion of a national (or multinational in pluriethnic countries) society be recuperated?

To understand development processes more broadly, it would be an error to think that everything can be reduced to formulae and mechanisms of accumulation. Accumulation is not coterminous with development; rather, it is just one of its components. The experience of the East Asian economies — which entered into severe economic crises in 1997, initially provoked through their financial systems — demonstrates the degree to which models of development, even capitalist ones, can differ from an open economy. In many respects, even as the old model has largely been abandoned, as discussed above, Latin America has not consciously confronted its future and remains some distance from defining an effective new model of development.

The so-called structural adjustments in various parts of the world played a central role in breaking with the old model of development. Time has shown that three distinct dimensions lie behind these adjustments. The first is a set of measures destined to resolve an immediate crisis, such as foreign debt, inflation, and fiscal deficit, which are symptomatic of a long-range problem like a loss of economic dynamism. The second is the mechanism by which the rupture with the old model occurs and the medium- and long-term transition from one model to the next. The end result is to make the economic sphere increasingly more independent of the political sphere, even though the transition is a process controlled by political actors. Third, the ideological dimension elevates short-term instrumental measures above the desideratum of a mere adjustment mechanism or even development model to the very definition of a desirable society and converts the market into its single paradigm. Neoliberalism has sought to fill this ideological role.

Neoliberal thought and practice have been associated with the structural adjustments of trade liberalization and privatization and, in turn, have been identified with a societal model of long standing. Most observers, except for the most fanatical neoliberal defenders, recognize that these theories and practices have fallen well short of their promise.[55] This does not mean that adjustments are not strictly necessary in certain moments of economic history, such as at the breakpoint of the statist-national-popular SPM in twentieth century Latin America. Structural adjustments had to resolve many of the region's short-term problems, prepare the groundwork for long-term growth, and contribute to the greater separation between politics and economics. In many countries, however, these technical measures have been taken as definitive models and have signified an increase in absolute poverty, skewed income distribution, and disrupted the state's and social actors' capacities to perform, which are key issues for a long-term model of development. The new relations among the state, social, and political actors are far from self-evident and cannot be defined simply by adjustment policies or neoliberal ideology.

What is clear is that the nexus between globalization and domestic trends and processes has generated not only the new economic trends discussed above but also has fostered new political, social, and cultural realities that are crucial to understanding the tensions and contradictions that confront a potential, effective new model of development and sociopolitical matrix that would be more economically viable, politically democratic, socially progressive, and culturally genuine.[56] If economic growth has been undergoing dramatic change, so have political and social trends and understandings of modernity, all of which help define development. Understanding these changes in the current period and how they interact with each other represents a challenge for social scientists trying to design appropriate explanatory and predictive categories.

POLITICAL DEMOCRATIZATION

Influenced by international pressures and currents of thought as well as by domestic processes and responses, the construction of political democracies of various types became the central political issue of the 1980s in the region and remained central through the 1990s.[57] Nations strove to establish a nucleus of democratic institutions to meet the basic needs of all regimes: form of government, definition of citizenship, and institutions to channel demands and resolve social conflicts.

The emergence or in some countries the reemergence of political democracy was also associated throughout the region with economic crises that in many cases eroded the fiscal basis of the state. These crises paved the way for privatization of state enterprises in many countries, while profoundly weakening the state's ability to satisfy basic functions. As a consequence, basic stateness in many countries deteriorated sharply and — when combined with the consequences of economic globalization discussed above — meant that the scope of political activities processed through state institutions declined and became less relevant.[58]

Thus, by the mid-1990s, political democracy prevailed throughout Latin America to a historically unprecedented degree. More countries satisfied the basic, if minimalist, criterion of being ruled through democratic elections than at any other time in the region's history. Yet, since their transitions over the past decade, some of these democracies had experienced declines and others oscillations regarding the extent to which basic civil rights or even political liberties were respected and deterioration in the quality of political representation. Profound questions remain regarding the type of political democracy being established, and these regimes' abilities to govern effectively and to promote economic growth and social equity.[59]

It is useful to begin by distinguishing among different types of political democratization. Analysts should avoid the pitfall of concluding that Latin America is simply riding a new, "third wave" of democratization around the world, a sweeping generalization that conceals important distinctions among different historical situations.[60] Granted, some contemporary processes of democratization do correspond to characteristics of previous historical periods, and all are affected at least to some extent by international forces and trends. However, practically all recent democratic transitions have responded mainly to domestic features and actors.

Since the 1980s, Latin America has witnessed three types of political democratization.[61] The first, "foundational," originates in a patrimonial or prolonged oligarchical system, typically comes about through popular and class struggles against traditional dictatorships, and is precipitated by revolution or civil war. This process of democratization is foundational in the sense that the democracy, however fragile and imperfect, is the first reasonably sustained and, in some cases, historical example in these societies of a system based on broad popular participation and representative institutions. Foundational democratization took place in several Central American countries — El Salvador and Nicaragua; with more complex historical patterns, Guatemala and particularly Honduras; and with somewhat different historical trajectories, the Dominican Republic and Paraguay. Typically, in this process there is a significant role for international actors and international mediation.

The second type, "transitional," occurs in societies governed by modern authoritarian regimes that previously possessed democratic governments and are now returning to that mode once again. It applies to countries with institutionalized military regimes, called by various authors bureaucratic authoritarian, new authoritarian, reactive foundational, or national security state. These we call democratic transitions because revolution or widespread insurrection does not accompany them, but they come about through different kinds of agreements or pacts between the democratic opposition and the authoritarian powerholders in order to restore democratic rules and eventually turn government back to civilians.[62] In this type, there is an extensive role for negotiation, as the armed forces retain varying degrees of control over the process and seek to defend certain prerogatives as well as to protect their impunity from punishment for the human rights violations they carried out while they were in power. The description is most apt for Southern Cone countries (Argentina, Chile, and Uruguay) and Brazil but also lends itself to Bolivia and Peru in the 1980s and 1990s.

A third type of political democratization, "democratizing reform," describes constrained democracies or semiauthoritarian systems that are governed by civilians. Rather than a formal regime change or democratic "inauguration," this process is one of extension of democratic principles and procedures. An institutional transformation advances some or all of the following: it incorporates excluded groups into the democratic game, configures an effective multiparty system, and/or facilitates expression of the popular will. Mexico is the best example of this type of political democratization; it was also attempted in Colombia in the early 1990s.

With regard to what has been termed democratic consolidation, the conceptual panorama is complicated because nearly all of these political democratizations are incomplete yet consolidated: incomplete because they lack full representation and democratic guarantees and consolidated because it is difficult to foresee an authoritarian regression.[63] And, if authoritarianism returns, it will come about as the result of some new crisis and not due to machinations by old authoritarian actors. Many dramatic events over the last two decades, such as substantial military rebellions in Argentina and Venezuela and forced presidential resignations in Brazil, Peru, Venezuela, and Argentina, did not lead to military coups, an outcome that foreseeably could have occurred in previous periods.[64]

While one of the three types of political democratization — foundational, transitional, or democratizing reform — may define the basic nature of democratization in any single country, elements of all three are typically present in each case. While the Argentine and Bolivian cases can be characterized as transitions, they also had foundational dimensions to the extent that they put an end to hybrid forms of authoritarianism and democracy or to frequent shifts back and forth between the two. The Paraguayan case combines foundational and transitional dimensions by closing the door on various decades of authoritarian rule. While Uruguay is close to a pure transition, Chile is an example of an incomplete transition followed by a process of reform still underway. Peru passed through a typical transition in 1975 to 1980, only to be followed by an authoritarian regression in 1993, a process of extension, and then renewed regression and reform over 2000-2001. While Colombia started a reform process in the early 1990s, following subsequent processes of violence and state decomposition, it now demands attention to foundational dimensions of democratization as well.

Foundational democratization often occurs in the wake of extensive violence or following prolonged dictatorial rule. Because it unleashes blocked political expression over many decades, it is naturally associated with brusque changes in all social spheres — cultural, economic, and ideological. In turn, transitions and reforms do not necessarily imply a confluence of such dramatic discontinuities in these other spheres. They are more purely political changes that can influence other socioeconomic, cultural, and international spheres that maintain their relative autonomy. Nor are transitions and democratizing reforms simply consecrations of the market economy, as some analysts of post-communist regimes or ideologues claiming the "end of history" would have us believe. Nevertheless, contemporary democratization in Latin America does appear to be associated with a shift in the sociopolitical matrix.

Transitions come about as a reaction against a particular type of military authoritarianism. The central characteristic of the regimes eclipsed by the transition was that the military institution assumed political power. The military and its allies spearheaded a dramatic reaction and severe repression against the prevailing statist-national-popular SPM, tried to nullify social mobilization as a political force, and favored a capitalist revival and reinsertion into the world economy. The end result was that, while they succeeded in dismantling politically mobilized or insurrectional social sectors, these regimes failed to eradicate the residual political actors from the old democratic system and, except in the Chilean case, failed to generate a new economic model. Rather than give birth to a new SPM, their main accomplishment was to disarticulate the statist-national-popular SPM.

Two factors coincided as the transitions evolved. First, the inability of the military dictatorships to generate a permanent and legitimate political regime induced them to appeal to "democratic mechanisms" in order to legitimate themselves. Thus, they either announced triumphantly that they had accomplished their mission or conceded (at least to themselves) that they failed and scrambled to maintain as many prerogatives as possible under reemergent democratic forms. Second, in every case, political and social mobilization contributed to force or reinforce an opening from above. These transitions were always preceded by negotiations and mobilization,[65] a complex political fencing game of thrusts, feints, and stabs played out on an institutional mat, which would end with continuation or termination of the regime.[66]

In these cases, never was the military defeated domestically as an institution, although the Argentine military was defeated externally. In some cases, the military command did suffer an internal reversal, as in Peru, and in all cases it was weaker after years of governance than it was immediately after its initial coup. The relative strength of the military as it relinquished power initially determined how well it could impose restrictions on the democratic institutions that followed, for example, regarding their ability to fend off prosecution of military wrongdoing while in power.

As a consequence, none of these countries at the end of transitions was able to achieve complete democratic civilian control over the military, which, to a greater (as in Chile) or a lesser (as in Argentina) extent, established various mechanisms or "authoritarian enclaves."[67] Transition challenges typically confronted by the new democratic governments included the need to overcome these mechanisms or enclaves to reduce the risk of an authoritarian regression and to maintain the alliance of democratic forces that would naturally tend to split and splinter in the face of electoral competition. Aside from differing perspectives on how to deal with the failure to punish the military's past human rights violations, divisive issues for the alliance were the definition of modernization and social democratization, how far to pursue structural adjustment and economic reforms, and who would pay for alleviating social inequities. Each of these questions raised different, sometimes contradictory, policy options.

Democratic foundations and reforms share some of the same features as democratic transitions. The fact that foundations often occur amid revolution or civil war makes it difficult for the players to move smoothly to a system of government that assumes those in power and those in the opposition respect each other as adversaries rather than enemies. The setting for foundational democracy in Central America has been at the end of prolonged civil wars, and negotiations between the two sides have usually required outside mediation, including for the first time since its establishment, the United Nations.[68] The construction of a democratic form of government is extremely slow. The revolutionary regime or first elected government after a civil war plays the part of a transitional government, which is not the same as a government in a democratic transition. The revolutionary regime and/or excombatants have to undergo a complex and painful metamorphosis into democratic political parties that end up in government or the opposition, abiding by new rules of behavior requiring tolerance and compromise. Nicaragua, El Salvador, and Guatemala after their respective peace processes are illustrative cases.

Democratic reforms emanating from the regime and the dominant party(ies) in power imply efforts to retain political and institutional continuity. The dominant political actors try to orchestrate change without surrendering power by implementing various electoral and political reforms. One result is that the structural transformations deriving from longer-term social changes or from short-term structural adjustments or crises, detonated by other factors such as drug trafficking, do not synchronize well with the political system. This clash or lack of synchronicity deepens the crisis of government without providing easy answers. The Mexican case appears to be moving toward a more felicitous outcome, following the defeat of the PRI first in congressional and then in presidential elections, and the relative success of the Fox administration in managing the country's many challenges. In contrast, the Colombian case remains far more indeterminate.[69]

In general, the processes associated with new democracies and the end of formally authoritarian or military regimes have played out while reforms are still underway. While a new wave of military dictators is unlikely, these processes of political democratization, through different paths, have shaped incomplete democracies with authoritarian enclaves, unrepresentative institutions, social actors distrustful of democracy, and ethical stigmas, such as unresolved human rights violations left over from the military governments. In some cases, regressions have occurred: Peruvian President Alberto Fujimori's 1992 *auto-golpe* (self coup) and his reelection in the fraudulent elections in 2000, even if short-lived, provide dramatic examples. In other cases, countries have adopted an unstable formula or a "situation," borrowing a phrase from Juan Linz, that combines both authoritarian and democratic elements.[70]

Yet, unlike the most recent, less complete, and more ephemeral "democratic moment" on the continent, in the late 1950s and early 1960s, currently no alternative international ideological model to democracy resonates in the region. Moreover, there are international organizations and social forces promoting democracy that did not exist or were much less influential three decades ago. Ideologically, there is no other model of rule competing with democracy in Latin America. Islamic fundamentalism lacks the religious adherents to be viable, and another potential competitor — built around a local variant of Asian authoritarianism — also lacks key cultural carriers or social bases and lost further viability due to the economic crisis that region entered into in 1997. The Cuban Revolution, which had such a profound impact on actors across the entire ideological spectrum, inspiring or strengthening guerrilla movements, counterinsurgency doctrines, and reformist impulses, especially in the 1960s, no longer serves as a model in the region.[71] With the end of the Cold War, both "single-track" antidemocratic policies and what had occasionally been "dual track" U.S. diplomacy, with intelligence and security elements pursuing hard-line policies independent of civilian diplomats, have moved toward a consensus around promoting democracy, understood particularly in electoral and free-market terms.[72] With a MERCOSUR democracy clause incorporated into the treaty following the successful efforts by Brazil and Argentina (among other countries) to thwart a 1996 coup attempt in Paraguay, the Brazilian and Argentine governments again played an important role in preventing military intervention after the 1999 resignation of President Raúl Cubas of Paraguay. Through the Organization of American States (OAS), there have also been steps toward establishing a multilateral framework for defending political democracy in the hemisphere. One such timid step was the passage of Resolution 1080 in 1991, which was invoked four times over the 1990s (in Haiti in 1991, Peru in 1992, Guatemala in 1993, and Paraguay in 1996). This was followed by slightly stronger measures, including passage of the Inter-American Democratic Charter in Lima, Peru, on September 11, 2001. This Charter defines the basic elements of democracy and establishes procedures for the OAS to carry out not only when democracy has broken down, but also when it appears to be at serious risk.

Beyond the actions of states and intergovernmental organizations, there is also an emerging transnationalism of new social movements and sometimes dense networks of linked international and domestic NGOs that can give sustenance to social movements struggling for democracy, human rights, or the extension of democratic and civil rights.[73] One indicator would be the forging of international networks in support of human rights, such as those that led to the arrest of Chilean General Augusto Pinochet in the Great Britain. Another would be the important UN-sponsored summits on women, the environment, education, human rights, and social policy — all of which have had important complementary participation by organizations from civil society.

As discussed in the previous chapter, other international economic changes bode less well for democracy. Policies to attract short-term capital inflows serve to finance budgetary and trade deficits; they simultaneously apply deflationary pressures on local producers. When a regime can move decisively to streamline the state structure and virtually eliminate the fiscal deficit, these policies can work. However, when they greatly exacerbate income gaps or are imperfectly implemented, the cost for democratic institutions may ultimately be unsustainable. Argentina under former President Carlos Saúl Menem and then in the context of the crisis that forced the premature resignation of his successor, President Fernando de la Rúa, is an example. As amply demonstrated in the cases of Mexico and Brazil in the 1990s, dependence on short-term borrowings can backfire when investors lose faith in the political regime or its ability to manage the state's economy. The ensuing financial reversals did not usher in new authoritarian regimes but reinforced popular skepticism of the new democracies. Export-oriented development strategies may well lead to fragmentation rather than integration of national economies, as a transnational integration based on geographical specialization and global sourcing emerges. Former ISI policies established a pattern of national segmentation. With the shift to EOI, Latin American states can at best hope to facilitate external investment, rather than intervene or act more directly; yet, they remain to a great degree at the mercy of state policies (for example, the degree and nature of protectionism) in consuming or importing countries.

At the international level, the profound economic transformations occurring on a global scale have helped to weaken Latin American states and severely attenuate the organizational capacities of numerous middle-sector and working class groups, while enhancing the strength and negotiating abilities of global and domestic financial conglomerates. The organizational weaknesses of these popular sector groups may have helped democratic transitions by easing the fears of the economically powerful regarding the risks of challenge and polarization. However, the organizational decline of these groups combined with sustained or growing gaps in wealth have profound implications for the basic stability, not to mention the quality, deepening, and relevance, of democratic rule. For example, largely absent have been effective alliances of civil society organizations and business groups around such common concerns as improved education, anticorruption, natural resource management, causes of criminality, judicial reform, and fiscal responsibility.

At the domestic level, key political and economic actors prefer the idea of democratic rule to a return to authoritarian military regimes, with the partial exception of upper and middle class support for a military coup against Venezuelan President Hugo Chávez. This preference subsists, even as what is meant by and what is possible under democracy come under continuous scrutiny. The major direct challenges that might lead to democratic breakdown thus have not recently come from the economically privileged, with the

Venezuelan exception, or from the very top ranks of the military, with the Paraguayan exception. In some cases, the "pro-regime" calculations of these groups obviously cannot be isolated from the international factors noted above (such as international pressures on President Jorge Serrano Elías to forestall an *auto-golpe* in Guatemala). Rather, the weakness and even disrepute of central political institutions and social actors have enhanced the ability of civilian leaders and middle-level military officers to appeal to popular support to carry out undemocratic actions. Examples are the *carapintadas* ("painted faces") commando units led by middle-ranking officers who rebelled over 1987-1990 in Argentina; President Fujimori's *auto-golpe* in 1992; the *bolivarianos* (members of the Movimiento Bolivariano Revolucionario or Revolutionary Bolivarian Movement, led by Lt. Colonels Hugo Chávez and Francisco Arias Cárdenas, who attempted a popular but unsuccessful coup d'état on February 4, 1992) in Venezuela; and in a somewhat different context, military officers sympathetic to socioeconomic protestors in Ecuador in 1998. Thus, the return to democratic politics is taking place in a context marked not simply by an observable break with previous military rule, but also by a continuity of historical patterns that lurk beneath the surface in many societies, some of which are disturbingly authoritarian in nature.

Political parties reemerged during political democratization after a long period during which authoritarian governments dismantled them or tried to reduce them to irrelevance. Although marked by the authoritarian interlude, there were also in many cases important historical continuities regarding the nature of the region's parties and party systems. When transitions were negotiated, the principal interlocutors for the "democratic bloc" were the political parties. This task, followed by their role of governing or being the opposition in the restored democracies, implied significant changes.[74] In some cases, the political class went through a collective learning process, often uneven or sometimes not very durable, on such themes as the nature of the dictatorships and the means of ending their institutional rule. In others, the lesson to be learned was how to move from political party cannibalism to cohabitation with other political groupings in arrangements that little by little came to resemble true party systems. This challenge was especially notable in those countries where a hegemonic party or a two-party system dominated and did not represent the whole society (examples are Argentina, Uruguay, and Paraguay.) The most significant outcomes were the partial renovation of existing parties with less emphasis on ideology, parties' increased interactions, and the emergence of new parties completing the spectrum. In countries where the political class failed to undergo a learning process, the results were tragic because an important segment of the political spectrum was practically pulverized. These cases opened up the greatest possibilities for authoritarian regression or democratic decomposition, as was especially evident in Peru and is becoming more apparent in the Venezuelan case. More complex to understand,

Argentina under President Menem, and more profoundly during the crisis of 2001-2002, provides another dramatic example of decomposition.

The discredited military regimes, in a rear-guard action, departed government trying to maintain their prerogatives, corporate privileges, and institutional identities. Their corroded identities could not be repaired by replicating previous missions to defend the national territory (nineteenth century); military developmentalism (1930s); protection of the middle classes (1950s); or new professionalism and/or national security ideology (1960s and 1970s).[75] A call for "national defense" was not particularly compelling in a global world, where threats can be as much environmental as military.[76] As political discourse has been largely empty of new directions for the armed forces — beyond vague calls for modernization, professionalism, and involvement in international peacekeeping missions — what is left for them to do except to provide security for individual citizens against crime and to combat the drug trade? Democratizing societies find these assignments to be dangerous to turn over to the military when new governments are trying to strengthen civil liberties and eradicate corruption. One positive option is to consider the establishment of a regional Latin American military with a mission focused on assisting the United Nations in peacekeeping operations and in other areas of collective security.[77]

The predominance within political discourse of economic themes, such as free markets, deregulation, trade liberalization, and state shrinking, does indeed have implications for the military, as they are part of the state apparatus that is being trimmed. The trend toward dispatching multinational peacekeeping forces to trouble spots throughout the world undermines the need for large national armies commanding huge resources. The new situation also raises questions about the viability of military industries, which require a certain minimal level of national procurement as well as the priority of developing military technology, when most nations' civilian scientific agendas, starved of funding, are more directly conducive to economic growth.

These various trends have led to occasionally dramatic shifts in the nature of civil-military relations in each country following a democratic transition, rather than to a smooth evolution toward greater civilian control.[78] Efforts to generate more contact with civilians and more effective civilian oversight of militaries have not always been fully effective. In Venezuela in the 1990s, as in Peru in the 1960s, contact with civilians led the military to seek more, not less, intervention in politics. The debate over the future of the Latin American military — its size, regulation, and resources — has often been defensive and contentious, and neither civilian nor military elites have articulated a vision of a viable long-term project.

The traditional fear of military intervention in politics in the form of actual or threatened coups has receded. At the same time, military prerogatives and effective military autonomy remain very high in many Latin American countries. Among the most significant changes is that military intervention does not have substantial support from international actors, powerful social sectors, or the military command, who are often dependent upon economic elites for their cues. This means that when coups are attempted, they are likely to fail, as in Argentina, Paraguay, and Venezuela, or to be short-lived, as in Ecuador. Calls for intervention have been muted in the absence of a perceived "threat" from below, with obvious exceptions, as in Colombia, or because of a conviction that the military would likely "mismanage" the economy more so than civilians. Those turbulent political situations in which military intervention would certainly have occurred in previous decades but did not in the contemporary period have simply added to the armed forces' isolation and perplexity.[79]

As the transitions came to a close, questions were asked about what sort of democracies were emerging in Latin America. Analysts responded by stressing their diverse and frequently defective forms, calling them, among other things, "delegative," "low intensity," or "electoral."[80] These democracies have inherited serious problems from their periods of transition, though their contemporary challenges can best be described now in terms of deepening, relevance, and quality. Democratic deepening refers to the extension of democratic procedures and ethical principles to other spheres of social life. Relevance refers to the extent to which major societal issues are channeled through and resolved by the democratic regime and its procedures rather than by de facto powers within the state, such as the military, or within society. The quality of democracy is related to expanding the scope of citizenship through participation, representation, and popular involvement in decisionmaking at the local, regional, and national levels. It is in terms of the responses to these challenges that the destiny of Latin American democracies will be decided in the foreseeable future.

SOCIAL DEMOCRATIZATION

Social democratization in Latin America has always been the ethical principle behind political democratization, but it should not be confused with it. There are three major issues related to social democratization. One relates to the problem of achieving social cohesion in the face of exclusion and fragmentation. Another refers to the expansion of citizenship and the need for institutions that can adequately express it. The third issue relates more broadly to participation.[81]

Social cohesion or social integration is currently being reconceptualized to take into account the new socioeconomic model in a globalized world system. International trends common across industrialized countries and the Latin American region include the spread of job informality and insecurity and social disintegration and crime in large urban areas. The impact of these trends is felt more intensely than in the industrialized countries because of their much higher overall levels, compounded by lower income levels and frayed safety nets, further shredded by the state fiscal crisis and reduction in welfare expenditures.

The faltering growth strategy of the 1970s led to the loss of state and industrial dynamism in the 1980s, which profoundly altered social stratification and mobilization. These had been favorite subjects of sociological research in the 1960s, and recent studies are only beginning to help us know the full human effects of the prolonged economic crisis and restructuring processes that continued into the 1990s.[82] Fairly obvious consequences have been the segmentation and informalization of social institutions, heightened precariousness of daily life, and in many countries the worsening of income distribution and poverty levels.

Indeed, at the turn of the century, Latin America as a whole has greater disparities of income distribution than any other region in the world. Historically, these disparities have been extremely high, though they improved modestly in the period leading up to the 1982 debt crisis, after which they once again tended to deteriorate. As reported by the Inter-American Development Bank (IDB), the region's Gini coefficient (a measure of income inequality that ranges from a high of 1 to a low of zero) fell by around 10 percent over the period from 1970 to 1982, and the share of low-income groups improved by around 10 percent, while that of the highest income groups fell or remained the same. Yet, all these gains were lost over the 1980s, as the top decile of the region saw its income share increase by over 10 percent, and the poorest decile experienced a drop of 15 percent in its income share.[83] Over the 1990s, most Latin American countries experienced no improvement in income distribution, and several saw even further deterioration. The patterns across income groups were marked by important differences across the region. However, of the 13 countries in Latin America supplying information for 1990 and 1999, in eight of them the income ratio between the top decile and the bottom four deciles grew even more, in one it remained the same, and in only four did it show improvement. At the decade's end, of 17 countries in the region, those with the worst Gini coefficients (over 0.55) included Bolivia, Brazil, Chile, Colombia, Guatemala, Nicaragua, Panama, and Paraguay; in turn, Uruguay (0.44) and Costa Rica (0.47) had the most equal distributions in the region.[84] Furthermore, although data limitations are even more severe with regard to issues of crime and violence, available statistics indicate that Latin America has one of the highest rates in the world for crimes such as homicide, and household surveys in major cities confirm widespread views that victimization rates are extraordinarily high. For example, over 50 percent of urban households in Guatemala and around 40 percent of urban households in Mexico and Ecuador report having been victims of some type of crime.[85]

The first expression of these changes is exclusion, which is best understood as a cleavage between those who are integrated into the material and symbolic attributes of the nation and those who are basically excluded from them, who remain impoverished, stigmatized, marginal, or repressed. The themes of exclusion/integration and fragmentation/cohesion have been at the core of Latin American social and national identities. In the contemporary context, when allusions are made to exclusion, the reference is to sectors that can make up one-third, one-half, or even a majority of the population who remain practically on the outside of society, just surviving and reproducing. Those large sectors of society who are excluded are not necessarily exploited or even necessary for the livelihood of the groups more successfully integrated into the global economy. Nor are the excluded groups composed basically of those previously integrated who experienced a relative decline in the security of their position. Excluded individuals and groups often cut across all social categories and identities, such as occupation, education, gender, region, rural or urban settings, and ethnicity. As a consequence, their possibilities of effective collective action have been sharply curtailed. Following current development models, it is simply not clear when and how many of these excluded groups will be successfully integrated.

Another aspect of the first problem is how to achieve social cohesion, given the fragmentation brought about by global production patterns. "National" development in Latin America always concealed disparities across regions. However, patterns of disparate development have been accentuated over the past decade with decentralization only partially and ineffectively redressing the inequities, indeed, in some cases even exacerbating them. Furthermore, interwoven with this kind of inequality is the one produced by the global patterns of production described above, minimized only partially by internal and international migration.

The collapse of the old model has had dramatic consequences for all the social groups associated with the statist-national-popular SPM, including middle and working classes and popular sector groups. Exaggerating only somewhat, one could assert the sociological disappearance of the middle class, which was the principal beneficiary of the industrialization, urbanization, and statist policies of that SPM. Proclamations of purely individual economic success have begun to erode the ideologies of meritocracy and *mesocracia* (rule by the middle class). The reduction in the size and functions of the state, the transformation of higher education into private training institutes for elites in the modern and growing transnational sectors, and an effective abandonment of the system of public education threaten social mobility for the popular sectors and the middle class.[86] With their structural, institutional, and value bases eroded, the trend increasingly is for the middle classes to be transformed into middle strata, essentially differentiated by their access to consumption. A few are able to become integrated into the high-income groups linked to services and employment in the transnational sector, while the majority find themselves poorer and increasingly marginalized. A thin social layer subsists as a vestige of the old middle class, but it is economically vulnerable and lacks a coalescing ideology. The growing insecurity of urban life creates continuous anxiety among these middle segments, resembling the situation that always affected the excluded popular sectors.

The consequences of exclusion and fragmentation have also severely impacted the capacity for collective action of other popular sectors. The organized working class has been weakened in nearly all countries in the region, and attempts by workers to regain their voice and their capacity for protest remain uneven. In a number of countries, the peasantry has diminished as a social category, to be replaced by temporary workers. In others, important peasant mobilizations, sometimes centered around ethnic identities, as in Mexico and Ecuador, or around basic demands for land, as in Brazil, have occurred as a reaction to these negative consequences.

For their part, the new economically dominant sectors have become closely linked to the central elements of the transnational socioeconomic model. Featured in international business and glamour magazines, they have hooked onto the most profitable and speculative elements of the model, such as privatizations and financial markets. A few opportunists have fed off its decomposing underside, such as various forms of corruption or narco-trafficking, and are pursued by law enforcement agents, some of whom are also corrupt. While privatization, finance, and corporate acquisitions have been where the action is and where money has been made, the participants are more loyal to their own business deals and their international interlocutors than to national development. The practice of philanthropy is underdeveloped, and the degree of social responsibility these people feel for dispossessed elements of their societies is disappointingly low, even among those who understand that social deterioration over the long term is bad for business. As such, these new rich have not yet constituted themselves as a true establishment or ruling class.

Lacking then, is any structural, value-based, or class "glue" that advances social integration and national unity. At most, in many countries in the region, public policy concerns are focused on the "poorest of the poor" through welfare (*asistencialismo*), based on narrow targeting and the principle of equity. Equity, however, in contrast to equality, is based on the idea that something must be done for those falling below a certain threshold. Public policies assign a corrective and subsidiary function to the state, not one of integral national development. Yet, social democratization is not possible without a focus on equality and redistribution — at the very least in terms of opportunity — although under conditions of political democracy this cannot be pursued through coercion. At the same time, the broad consensus that would be required has been difficult to accomplish in a political democracy.

The expansion of citizenship together with the need for appropriate institutions is the second issue related to social democratization. Citizenship was initially defined in ancient Greece as the recognition of a subject's rights in the face of public power within a territorial "polis," the classical space for citizenship. Later, the notion of "polis" spread outward to include economic and social rights. Today, gender relations, the mass media, the environment, and the workplace have come to constitute new spaces for contesting the rights of citizenship. People want to be citizens not just to have a minimum salary or political and civil rights, but also to obtain acceptance for additional rights as they define them. These claims, however, are not always recognized by public authorities or political institutions and not only in Latin America. While the concept of citizenship is becoming broader, it must deal with new exclusions, due, among other reasons, to the weakness of traditional actors and institutions and the absence of new ones where these new claims of citizenship may be channeled.

A third issue related to social democratization is the phenomenon of participation, in terms of the degree of democracy prevalent locally and in other territorial spaces, as well as in functional areas. Participation in Latin America has traditionally connoted either "access to" those in power or mobilization. Because mobilization is more difficult to achieve in the current socioeconomic context, participation is currently defined more in terms of "access to" with a focus on quality of service, as well as more in terms of representation than mobilization. Thus, in areas as diverse as health, education, work, information, and decisionmaking, questions of access are combined with demands about quality, blurred by issues of social stratification. Not surprisingly, this complicates even more the ability of the state to formulate and implement public policies.

THE MODEL OF MODERNITY

Without using the term, social actors express themselves partially in terms of their modernity, whose definition and meaning can arouse fervent debate among intellectuals.[87] As noted earlier, we understand modernity to be the manner in which a society constitutes its subjects, with subjects being those citizens capable of constructing their own history. The absence of modernity in a society is the virtual absence of autonomous subjects, either individual or collective. Sociologically, we cannot speak of a single modernity — but of various different modernities. Each society embodies its own diverse set of modernities. The different models of modernity involve combinations of three different elements: a rational scientific-technological dimension; an expressive-subjective dimension (feelings, emotions, drives); and collective historical memory.

The socioeconomic changes currently affecting Latin America have led the particular forms of Latin American modernity to enter into crisis, causing competing new models to confront each other. The new model of modernity that is most insistently laid out is one that posits structural adjustment as a path to an ideal society, which identifies modernity worldwide with historical modernization in the industrialized world and reduces social interactions to economic exchanges. This model is condemned to failure despite its popularity among some Latin American elites. It does not take into consideration the existence of national and group identities, ignores collective memory, excludes the majority of the people, denies the role of politics, and lacks national social actors who can fully implement it.

An alternative vision is represented by a new version of Catholic corporatism or integralism. To an excessively rationalist Western modernity, this model presents as an alternative an essentialist subject with a purported Latin American identity, centered in a Christian people represented by the Catholic Church, ostensibly created in the process of the conquest and evangelization of the region over 500 years ago. This kind of thinking, associated with Pope John Paul II, can have a degree of social legitimacy, as it contains certain progressive socioeconomic views regarding currently excluded social sectors and also condemns the materialism, inequalities, and immoralities of the capitalist economy and the market. However, this vision is profoundly reactionary with regard to sociocultural issues and has an antirationalist and antilibertarian bias.

In general terms, the first structural adjustment model tends to reduce modernity in Latin America to a rationalist-technological view, in imitation of certain industrialized countries, whereas the integralism model reduces it to an essentialist and meta-social identity that prevents the creation of true subjects. Between the two poles are a broad range of partial solutions, among them, models centered on media-generated mass culture, original identities, or particularistic communities. The region is currently in the midst of a debate — sometimes open, sometimes unspoken or hidden — about appropriate models of modernity for this era.[88]

As we have seen, globalization has affected the economic, political, social, and cultural dimensions. At the same time, as we explore in further detail in the next chapter, the vast changes in Latin America have also responded to domestic pressures and factors within and across each of these dimensions.

Chapter Five

TOWARD A MATRIX CHANGE

The growing contradictions experienced by the statist-national-popular SPM led to its emerging internal crisis. This crisis was expressed in the disjuncture between two options, one that sought to deepen its dependent-capitalist aspects with the concomitant reversion of its populist policies and another that focused on deepening social democratization with the concomitant replacement of its dependent-capitalist components. The new types of military regimes that emerged first in Brazil in 1964 and subsequently in other Southern Cone countries are an expression of the first option. The Popular Unity government of Salvador Allende in Chile (1970-1973); the late Peronism of Héctor Cámpora (1973); and, in its most extreme version, the guerrillas of the 1960s are expressions of the second option, ultimately violently defeated in almost all parts of the region.

The military dictatorships, followed by the processes of democratization, the phenomenon of globalization discussed in Chapter Three, and the structural reforms with which they were associated, all profoundly disarticulated the statist-national-popular matrix. In spite of the neoliberal efforts from within and without the region, a new stable matrix of relations between the state and society and their key components has not consolidated itself. On the contrary, what is apparent in the region are contradictory traits that combine, for example, a consolidation of democratic regimes with greater poverty and inequality, a growing political destructuring of collective behavior combined with increased activation of fragmented social movements, an increased institutionalization of political life joined with its declining relevance to the lives of people, and a growing expansion of markets with a weakening in collective decision-making capacity through the state.

A new sociopolitical matrix implies a coherent transformation of the development model, as well as of the key components of the matrix, the state, political institutions and a system of representation, social actors and their cultural orientations, and the political regime. Instead, what is occurring are tendencies in multiple and sometimes contradictory directions, with residual elements of the old juxtaposed with new ones, making it difficult to discern which trends represent temporary transitional phenomena and which will be longer lasting.

THE DEVELOPMENT MODEL

The new approaches to development in Latin America drew on the errors of the past, observations on what had worked elsewhere in the world, pressure from international agencies, and links to the region's historical legacy. Most influential was the economic crisis of the 1980s, even though its policy strands originated in the authoritarian governments of Chile and Argentina in the 1970s. However, to understand the new tendencies that seek to replace the previous development model, it is important to examine the problems and inefficiencies built into the old one that required its abandonment, the intellectual origins of the new tendencies, and the nature of the coalitions supporting the change.

Once Latin American political elites conceded that the old development approach needed to be modified or discarded, the evolution of these tendencies passed through at least three stages: 1) receptivity to specific policies to correct the most untenable features of the preexisting model (typically called "adjustment"); 2) movement toward a new growth strategy, including political and social features; and 3) infusing the strategy with an ideological or normative dimension. As was the case with ISI, the social, political, and ideological dimensions of any new model eventually needed to be intertwined.[89]

We have said that one dimension of adjustment policies was to eliminate economic distortions. The technical and ideological rationale of this policy was crystallized in the so-called "Washington consensus."[90] Privatization of state industries was proclaimed in order to free the central government (and monetary authorities) from paying their recurrent budgetary deficits and to place assets under the ownership of corporations and entrepreneurs with investment capability. Liberalization lowered tariff rates, freed the exchange rate, and eliminated exchange controls in order to spur competition, increase productive efficiency, and lower domestic prices. Monetary policy became restrictive to dampen inflation and included high interest rates to attract short-term foreign capital. Public sector reform reduced the number of state employees; sought to improve tax collection and to strengthen banking and credit supervision, after an initial experiment with extreme financial laissez-faire; and curtailed public services, such as health and education, to contract the public sector deficit. These policies set the stage for export-oriented production to integrate the nation into the global economy, earn foreign exchange, attract investment, and assure that national producers added value to production based on the country's comparative advantage.

These policy changes were not generated domestically but were based on particular worldwide currents of economic thought. Neoclassical and monetarist theorists had long considered the precepts of ISI to be counterproductive and recommended the above policies as the only route to long-term growth. The dramatic success of Asian economies in becoming links in buyer-driven and producer-driven global commodity chains (and in some cases generating their own commodity chains) reinforced these arguments. The key government officials managing the economies of major Latin American countries received their graduate degrees under the guidance of professors (mainly in the United States) whose economic theories were neoclassical or monetarist. International agencies such as the IMF and the World Bank promoted these policies timidly before 1982 and then aggressively through conditionality clauses in new loans after the debt crisis drastically weakened the capacity and will of Latin American states to resist. Transnational corporations simply let it be known that until tariff, foreign exchange, investment, and profit repatriation laws changed, they would make new investments in Asia, where growth rates were higher than in Latin America.

Local economic elites initially were divided over the new policies. The business groups that had cash reserves or easy access to international finance welcomed the new policies because they could walk away with the lion's share of privatized industries and compete efficiently in a less regulated environment. Leaders of industries whose profitability relied on tariff protection, subsidized inputs, and price controls were fearful of new competition. At the very least, they insisted on time to react to the changes, but in many countries as the crisis deepened, they found themselves incapable of blocking the new policies and resigned themselves to a less wealthy and prominent position in the private sector pecking order. The same happened with traditional agricultural sectors oriented toward the internal market. In the final analysis, the most immediately disadvantaged were the lower- and middle-income groups, which experienced price increases, job dismissals, and cuts in social services. In all cases, the adjustments caused severe increases in poverty, inequality, and social disintegration for an extended period.

Initially, regime type — authoritarian or democratic — determined whether these policies would be adopted. The first Latin American country to move decisively away from ISI, Chile, did so under an authoritarian military government and the second, Mexico, under an authoritarian civilian regime. These new policy initiatives, however, were not necessarily incompatible with elected regimes operating in democratic or semi-democratic systems, as demonstrated by later events. Between 1985 and 1995, Argentina, Uruguay, Venezuela, Peru, Colombia, Ecuador, Bolivia, Paraguay, and Brazil began the economic reform process under elected presidents and functioning congresses. In some countries, a technocratic elite, using authoritarian methods and skipping democratic consensus, enforced the policies. The atmosphere surrounding these policies included recognizing some of the dysfunctions of the previous economic model, mainly the subordination of the economy to political objectives; the dramatic decline of popular sector unions and political organization during the 1980s; hyperinflation; and the heightened status of capitalism worldwide with the collapse of the former Soviet Union. Popular class urban demonstrations in some countries protested the hardship these policies caused, and owners of ISI industries warned that unbridled imports would transfer national wealth abroad; yet, their combined opposition was insufficient to stem the momentum.

Many advocates of economic liberalism argued that an open, democratic system is the most congruent political environment for free markets and that free markets, in turn, eventually produce democratic systems.[91] The debate over the relationship between capitalism and democracy is extensive and cannot be resolved here. While consolidated democracy never has existed empirically in a command economy and is unlikely to do so because of limitations imposed on the maintenance of an independent civil society and the sustainment of a vibrant political opposition, neither has it existed with totally free, unfettered markets for equally compelling theoretical reasons: state power is required to establish and to maintain markets and to address market failures, and a democratic, responsive state must regulate markets in order to overcome the inequalities and fragmenting forces markets generate.[92] Thus, a simple, mutually supportive, causal relationship between the two is debatable, especially in intermediately developed capitalist systems. At least in Latin America, economic liberalism and political democratization have not followed a linear and cumulative path; indeed, they clearly have not always been mutually converging and reinforcing. The coincidence of economic liberalism and democracy in the 1980s and 1990s was a historical accident. A new economic model was essential in the 1980s because of the collapse of ISI. And, democracy returned to many Latin American countries in the 1980s after a long period of authoritarian military regimes. While the military's legitimacy petered out in part because of those regimes' economic failures and democratically elected governments have been the midwives of economic reforms, political democracy also acquired stronger legitimacy as international competitors declined, especially following the collapse of the Soviet Union and the end of the Cold War. This new context allowed democracy to survive in some countries under circumstances of crisis that in past periods would probably have led to renewed breakdown.

The new economic model placed a preponderance of responsibility on private enterprise for investment and growth. To justify the pursuit of profits in a competitive environment, the model's ideology predicted that private companies had incentives to utilize capital, natural resources, and labor as efficiently as possible. Lowering import barriers created competition from foreign producers and helped force the domestic private sector to "get the prices right." A country's export capability was based wholly on its comparative advantages in the world economy. State intervention was limited to monetary policy, tax collection, and prevention of fraud. A free market was said to be the guarantor of efficient resource allocation and prices, and regulations were to be minimal on foreign exchange, job protection, foreign investment, imports, and exports. Not all countries, of course, including Chile and Mexico, have followed all the measures implied by the theoretical model. And empirical questions exist as to whether even the successful Asian NICs were true to the dictates of the theory during their high-growth phase, particularly with respect to the role of the state.[93]

The new economic model in Latin America was incomplete as a development strategy without social, political, and ideological components. These associated features permitted the strategy's diffusion throughout society and reinforced and complemented the economic logic. Although the economic component of the development strategy was usually more obvious and measurable, its other features over the long term have been equally important. Societies do not live by economics alone. A fundamental question has been whether the new approach can solve the joint challenges of generating legitimacy and providing for its own reproduction. Successful reproduction depends not only on questions of growth but also rests on sustainable resource management, as Latin America bumps up against the limits of the region's ecological elasticity and demographic carrying capacity.

In the initial stages, domestic acceptance of Latin America's economic changes was facilitated by widespread despair over inflation and hyperinflation, low or even negative growth, corruption, unemployment, and decline in the quality of life — blamed by public opinion on the crisis and by the dominant elites on the previous economic system. For increasing sectors of the population, any change seemed preferable to the status quo. At the same time, incumbent governments or regimes did everything possible to blame the costs of the new economic model on their predecessors. For instance, in Chile during the military government, the authorities satanized the Popular Unity government of Salvador Allende, alluding to the economic and political chaos of that earlier period to mollify discontent with Pinochet's austerity policies. And, during his first term in office, President Menem in Argentina blamed the previous administration of Raúl Alfonsín for the problems he inherited and the international system for imposing certain measures upon him.

As economic adjustment has continued throughout Latin America in varying degrees, economic elites and very small segments of the middle class have begun to benefit in differing degrees and circumstances. When falling tariffs levels and privatization promised to transfer large portions of the national asset base from public to private hands, influential constituencies (mainly those in business positioned to take advantage) became enthusiastic advocates. The privatization process itself frequently led to enormous concentrations of wealth in the hands of a few private entrepreneurs. The opening to foreign investment spawned joint ventures managed by domestic executives who, generalizing from their own improved economic prospects, have claimed that the reforms are compatible with the national interest of their countries. Differentiation and specialization required by a more modern productive structure created some new middle-class jobs in accounting, law, information and communication, management, transportation, training, and technical research. As the economies gained momentum, demand for labor increased, moving from initially massive joblessness to large and hard pockets of unemployed, giving particular popular sectors a stake in the system. Social programs that were first cut back to reduce the public sector deficit were reformatted to provide limited benefits to specific groups in the form of a safety net or "targeted policies."

Ideally, a dynamic economy operating with nearly full employment, providing steady income gains for all social sectors, could create its own legitimacy. Problems arise when benefits are less generous or less widely distributed, fluctuate with the business cycle, or are curtailed after a financial or broader economic collapse. Unfortunately, after 1995 and particularly after 2000, this has been a too common occurrence. During 1995, as a consequence of the devaluation of the Mexican peso in December 1994, various countries in the region experienced significant capital outflows; ultimately, Mexico, Argentina, and Uruguay, in particular, were seriously affected. The Asian crisis that broke out in the second half of 1997, which was then exacerbated by the debt moratorium and devaluation in Russia in August 1998, particularly affected South American countries, as Mexico and Central America benefited from the strength of the U. S. economy. The 2001-2002 crisis, more global in nature, has had extensive implications for trade as well as finance.[94] The question facing national elites has been: What are the ideological pillars of legitimation for the new approach?

A common choice appears to be neoliberalism as an ideology, which has implications for the size and scope of the public sector, for individual rights and responsibilities, and for the promise of a market society in which all citizens can consume and produce whatever they want. The previous statist-national-popular model emphasized state initiative and collective values. According to those who espouse neoliberalism, the razing of traditional power centers in the state and in protected pockets of the economy purportedly creates multiple opportunities for individuals to maximize their potential through their own efforts, with fewer institutional, political, and social barriers. People at all income levels are told they can "make it" in the new economy by following conventional or fortuitous paths without help from government. If they fail, it is their own fault or bad luck. Those who succeed are to be the role models for their family, friends, acquaintances, and the acquaintances of their acquaintances. The stories of individuals who have significantly bettered their lives economically can have an inspirational effect on those who observe or learn of them. They believe they might do the same and do not blame the political system when they fail, but rather, their individual shortcomings. This demonstration effect of a few successful individuals is intended to help legitimize the system among the society at large, even for those who have not benefited. Elites choosing neoliberalism as an ideological prop for the new system are hoping to relieve the state of pressure to resolve all national economic and social problems

— without dispensing with state interventions needed to implement the model and to achieve specific (their own) economic and social goals.

It is unlikely, however, that this sort of neoliberal ideology will take root in Latin America, which has been less oriented toward individualism and more beholden to the state than have the small cluster of countries typically associated with liberal and neoliberal values. Moreover, successive financial crises and increasing rates of unemployment and job precariousness have totally discredited the neoliberal claims for legitimacy. The evolving Latin American ideology, which sets standards for individuals, families, categories and groups, and public authority, is certain to incorporate both individualistic and collective components.

While nationalism persists as a strong force in Latin America, its relevance for the emerging development model is different from its relevance for its ISI predecessor. Instead of restricting foreign investment, economic nationalism requires a defense of the country's economic interests in international treaties and accords. Instead of blocking the entry of foreign goods into local stores, the new economic model requires access for domestic production in foreign markets. The emotional effect of each approach on national pride is different and potentially more uplifting in the latter case. The purchase by industrialized economies of nontraditional Latin American exports elevates the worth of the exporting nation. The economic law of comparative advantage internationally spills over into the value of cultural diversity domestically. Folklore, dress, music, traditions, art, literature, collective behavior, and customs — the core of national identity — were always strong unifying symbols for popular sectors.[95] Under the new strategy, these same traits, except when politically oriented, may have a greater probability of being appreciated by economically powerful groups who previously rejected national traditions in favor of European or U.S. artifacts. These powerful groups' economic prospects are increasingly determined by their ability to compete internationally with unique national goods and services, particularly the tourism industry. In sum, Latin American elites can use nationalistic symbols — in nonhistorical, nonmobilizational, and nonpolitical ways — selectively as instruments for legitimation, unification, and consensus, as they were used under the previous development model.

Fully evolved, the most benevolent economic vision foresaw the new Latin American development model combining an economy based on some classical principles (such as competitiveness) with a limited productive and moderate regulatory role for the state, strong and differentiated international linkages with important roles for various regional and subregional groupings of countries, some weak publicly financed social programs targeted to the most needy groups, and programs with a soft notion of equity — all within a political regime legitimized by a type of social contract between the individual and the state. The social coalition backing the new strategy (that is, those individuals who would have the greatest potential to reap its rewards) would be the economic elites, particularly owners of privatized and export-oriented industries; the ascendant sectors of the middle class; the employed working class in the modern sector; and technocratic bureaucrats linked to private businesses. Foreign corporations would be receptive as long as their Latin American subsidiaries were useful components of their worldwide production or marketing strategies. International financial institutions would be supportive, conditioning their investments on the maintenance of the core elements of the model. The military would be observant and disengaged but wary of denationalization, particularly in strategic sectors such as minerals, petroleum, and telecommunications, and in the future of their own industries. This strategy would provide for each nation's economic renovation by subjecting it to competition in areas for which it claimed a comparative advantage, offering incentives to entrepreneurs to exploit new economic niches domestically and internationally and reformatting the state's coalition of political support.

Latin American countries have not formed a general, ethical, and ideological consensus that could support this new strategy as the future development model. Rather, partial agreements have been reached in some countries, sometimes implicitly, on some principles and measures. Simultaneously, this strategy has been criticized for its adverse effects on social integration, equality, the environment, and culture. Indeed, for it to succeed as a development model, some of these disharmonious outcomes would inevitably need to be corrected, thus transforming its very nature. Moreover, if sectors of the population seemed to accept the strategy, it was because of the lack of an alternative and not as the desideratum of a fundamentally better society, as neoliberals proclaim. Intellectuals and some institutions, such as the Catholic Church, are very critical of the model's cultural, social, and political effects but have been unable so far to put forward a fully developed alternative. At the same time, alternative plans have been emerging from a variety of perspectives. Without returning to the earlier development model, they seek to rescue the role of the state vis-à-vis an unrestricted focus on markets, to emphasize issues of sustainable and equitable development, and to proclaim an open regionalism for these countries in the face of globalization. There are also more radical anti-neoliberal or anti-globalization platforms with significant mass acceptance, expressed in such meetings as those of the World Social Forum, held annually in Porto Alegre, Brazil, for the last several years. It can be noted from the sources of the more orthodox and official statements of the Washington Consensus that some corrections and additions to the model have been emerging.[96]

In sum, the new economic strategy initially seemed to solve some important problems of the previous model concerning economic distortions. But with the turn of the century, there is little doubt that most Latin American countries that tried to follow the neoliberal market-driven agenda of structural reforms failed to achieve sustainable development. Not only have their long-run growth performances been disappointing in general, but huge wealth and income inequalities have usually accompanied their erratic growth. In fact, the few successful cases, like Chile, have tried to follow their own development strategies.[97] It is true that a revised and expanded version of the Washington Consensus appeared with a longer list of recommendations that included governance and other institutional reforms, but it basically shared the same problems of the first one and was irrelevant for practical development purposes. This criticism of the Washington Consensus does not mean that we are, in principle, against some of its recommendations, such as promoting fiscal discipline and sound monetary policy, favoring a more prominent role for markets in resource allocation, limiting rent-seeking behavior, and encouraging a deeper integration with the world economy. However, Latin American countries should do so taking into account their underlying political economy, their specific macroeconomic conditions, the scope of their external vulnerabilities, the development of their financial markets, and the structural imbalances of their fiscal accounts, as well as other significant market and coordination failures ingrained in their economies that most certainly demand the intervention of an efficient and effective state.

The new strategy associated with market-driven neoliberalism has liquidated the basis of the previous development model and has partially broken the subordination of the economy to politics. However, Latin America still has not devised a coherent new development model that helps insure productive relations between state and society. The creation of such a model and the construction of these relations is the main task ahead.

THE STATE AND POLITICAL INSTITUTIONS

The emergence of a new SPM relates not only to factors of production, social movements, and culture, but also to the political regime. Regimes with varying degrees of democracy have persevered at various levels of consolidation in most Latin American countries. Democratization potentially serves two functions, practical and ideological. Among their advantages, democratic arrangements allow the development model to evolve, faced with pressures while maximizing legitimacy for the system as a whole. Political parties, elections, congressional debates, regulated protests, and a relatively unfettered press provide the channels for expressing discontent and permitting self-correction of ill-conceived policies or their replacement. Democratic systems, which even in attenuated forms respond in some degree to popular sentiment, have mechanisms to correct economic reforms according to the social and political context. However, herein lies the most important challenge for Latin American democracies. Is it possible in the globalized world and with the pressures of transnational powers and international institutions like the IMF and the World Bank to implement national economic policies? And, if it is not possible or only possible in very limited and constrained ways, how can these regimes preserve the undisputed legitimacy of democratic institutions? The alternative — an authoritarian government as was the Chilean case during the Pinochet administration — would simply force the model down the throats of the populace. To the degree that the new approach emerges from the give-and-take of political competition and is perceived as such, it carries the legitimacy of having been "chosen" by the people, but complex social, environmental, and cultural constraints make this legitimation game very difficult and hardly guaranteed, in spite of a significantly changed international context.

In post-authoritarian Latin America, democracy has tended to lose the connotation it acquired during the statist-national-popular SPM, without being fully replaced by another alternative. In that period, by concentrating conflict resolution within the state, the regimes displayed their hybrid character, which combined both democratic and authoritarian elements. As such, the leaders' and peoples' commitment to democratic institutions was tenuous, and the institutions' contributions to governability were limited. The majority of the regimes that have recently undergone political democratization are now seeking a path beyond transition from dictatorship or hybrid regimes to overcome their legacies or enclaves and to transform themselves economically, which presupposes new relations between the state and social actors, involving major changes in the deepening, the relevance, and the quality of their democracies.

Government

Presidential authority is the distinctive element in the formal structures of Latin American democracy. Conflicts have revolved around several closely inter-related issues: the appropriate powers and authority of the president as a plebiscitarian figure, the nature of executive-legislative relations, and the ability of the judiciary to provide a constitutional check on the other branches of government in an independent, cogent way. These conflicts have reflected the broader struggles for power and influence in Latin American society, both within and outside constitutional parameters.

The economic crises of the last two decades led many presidents to rely heavily on the considerable rule-making and decree powers they had accumulated gradually over the decades. Executive latitude for action came through constitutional provisions, congressionally delegated authority, or simply de facto executive fiat, facilitated by a judiciary dependent upon the executive or by congressional abdication (for example, President Carlos Menem in Argentina, President Joaquín Balaguer in the Dominican Republic, and Presidents Miguel de la Madrid and Carlos Salinas de Gortari in Mexico). Stalemated executive-legislative relations in a crisis context also led presidents to employ special decree powers, though usually with less success (for example, President Fernando Collor de Mello in Brazil and President Raúl Alfonsín in Argentina). In Peru, President Alberto Fujimori filled the vacuum left by a discredited Popular American Revolutionary Alliance (Alianza Popular Revolucionaria Americana — APRA) and an aged political class. He used military support and then elections to convert the legislature into an extension of his political will. In a number of cases (such as President Menem in Argentina, President Fernando Henrique Cardoso in Brazil, and President Fujimori in Peru), presidents successfully modified constitutions in order to extend their terms in office.

Yet, a countertrend, exemplified by other constitutional reforms in the region and by presidential and congressional behaviors, has indicated a curbing of presidential prerogatives and the establishment of somewhat more balanced executive-legislative relationships, particularly when the president has lacked a clear partisan majority, as in Mexico first under President Ernesto Zedillo and then more clearly under President Vicente Fox, in the Dominican Republic under President Leonel Fernández, and in Brazil under President Cardoso. A particularly dramatic example of this countertrend was the ouster of President Abdalá Jaime Bucaram Ortíz by the Ecuadorian legislature in 1997. The extensive and continuous nature of constitutional and electoral reforms in the region, however, underscores how political actors' bitter struggles for power and for the resources that lie behind it overwhelm the decline of ideological politics and the declining capabilities of the Latin American state. Struggles over the formal rules — even as informal ones occasionally weigh more heavily — speak to the importance of these institutional issues.

Efficient relations between the executive and legislative branches and the attributions of one or the other should not be confused with the question of the form or system of government, though debates have been ongoing between the value of presidentialism or parliamentarism and their intermediate forms.[98] Beyond the technical questions involved, there are two core problems. One is how to constitute governing majorities in systems that have historically been presidential and multiparty. The other is how to achieve a more balanced set of constitutional prerogatives between the two branches, while insuring that Congress would have the will and the capacity to participate in policymaking and oversight in ways that are more than simply obstructionist or venal. The debate begins with the legitimate observation that presidentialism has at times been "excessive" and continues with the observation that alternative ways exist to build majorities, to make coalition governments resilient, and to imbue legislatures with capacity, accountability, and transparency. These can involve issues relating to the party system and the electoral system as well as constitutional, legal, and informal relations among the various branches of government.[99]

An appropriate balance between effectiveness and the ability to act on one side and democratic access and accountability on the other is necessary. The legislature must have sufficient prerogatives to be involved in key policy-making decisions and in providing oversight of actions by the executive. The legislature's inability to balance the executive at times reflects the absence of an independent judiciary, free of political manipulation, intimidation, underfinancing, and corruption, and capable of serving as an effective check on unconstitutional actions by the other branches. There is also the potential risk of a judiciary that is excessively insulated, legalistic, and unconstrained, and/or not organized appropriately to address constitutional matters in a clear and timely way. Yet, this inability may involve a real imbalance of powers between the executive and the legislative branches, embedded in constitutional texts and informal practices, in which clientelist or parochially oriented legislatures are content to have the executive alone promote national-level agendas. Such systems may endure for considerable lengths of time, especially if the executive is granted special legislative powers to confront crises, though this does not make them desirable.

The State

The words "state reform" are often a code for "state obliteration." The international debate over the reform of the state has been nourished by divergent ideological visions that initially included the idea of its virtual disappearance. Advocates of state reform later settled on notions of administrative decentralization; narrowing of functions; deregulation (which in practice meant conforming to the regulatory schemes of rich countries); reduction of expenditures and fiscal austerity; and state "modernization" through computerization and outsourcing. These visions consisted of only a partial view of the problem and did not encompass state reform as an integral process. The policies aiming toward state modernization contained strong antistate biases and a short-term mentality. The Latin American region has given primacy to administrative reforms that disarticulate the relations between government and society rather than those that would lead to a substantive transformation of the state.

The antistate biases that have come into vogue are ahistorical, empirically false, and frequently contradictory. One part of public opinion affirms the universal panacea of the market, while another demands an active role for the state as an agent for distribution and an axis for national unity. Yet another philosophical position elevates civil society as a protagonist to confront the state, while conveniently ignoring the relative weaknesses of social actors in Latin American society or the fragmentation of organizations in civil society.

The point of departure of new relations between the state and society is the historical fact that no contemporary national development has succeeded by omitting a predominant role for the state. It is true that we have come to the end of an epoch characterized principally by "inward looking" national development, in which the mobilizing state was the undisputed and sometimes unstoppable agent of change. While Latin America is witnessing the emergence of a development model closely linked to transnational market forces, this trend does not signal the insignificance of state action, but rather, the modification of its organizational forms of intervention and the redefinition of its relations with other social actors.

An examination of real cases of the state's insertion into the new sociopolitical matrix reveals that the principle of "stateness" is still valid. In some cases, the state is trying to create the matrix, and in others it is seeking to reinforce an emerging matrix's consolidation.[100] Indeed, "stateness" may now be a much more significant strategic issue than was the case under the statist-national-popular SPM. With the market playing a more significant integrating role, the state in Latin America now must use far more sophisticated mechanisms of inducing compliance and achieving coordination with societal and international actors; the constraints under which the state operates mean it cannot simply impose solutions. What is required, therefore, is not a simplistic reduction of the role of the state but its strategic modernization, as it seeks to provide a legitimate and democratic order, decentralize, reorganize participation, and remain a crucial agent of development. Attending to new problems or to new forms of old problems, like those relating to justice, human rights, environment, and especially overcoming poverty, fall into the category of government policy or "statism."

The decentralization of the state apparatus should not simply serve as a technical means to improve decisionmaking, however necessary that goal is. The real issues are local democracy, governmental forms, and regional autonomy, which should not be confused with privatization or a weakening of state power. In many Latin American countries, the national government has transferred state services to municipal authorities while maintaining a central vision of overall service and technical standards.[101] A practical purpose has been to relieve costs from the central state, reduce the fiscal deficit, and transfer responsibility for controlling cost overruns to local entities. A more important objective has been to resolve problems of party representation and assign a quota of public offices to power contenders, which strengthens municipal entities, local democracy, and national representation. The results of fiscal and political decentralizing reforms in countries such as Brazil, Chile, Colombia, and Venezuela have been decidedly mixed. In Brazil, programs were devolved to the regions without commensurate responsibilities for assuring their funding, causing severe consequences for governance. In Colombia and in Mexico, decentralizing reforms in various regions have degenerated into corruption and mismanagement due to the absence of trained personnel at the local levels, inappropriate mechanisms of state oversight, and/or a lack of independent organizations in civil society. In turn, in other regions in these countries and in other countries such as Uruguay, the popular election of mayors and other decentralizing reforms have provided for important new spaces of democracy and popular participation. The forms of local and regional participation and their connection with the central state will be one of the fundamental problems to be resolved in the new SPM.[102]

The ideologues of neoliberalism who favored severe structural adjustments were certain that the market, through subsequent economic growth, would automatically generate the needed resources to improve living standards. In country after country in the region, this simply has not occurred. The adjustments stripped away the safety net for the lower classes and many in the middle class. Addressing social problems requires specific policies implemented by committed leaders of coherent public institutions that distribute resources through social expenditures.

The idea of a "subsidiary state" (that is, one subordinate to the economy), which would operate during the first stages of the adjustment, brought with it a corollary of welfare policies for the most severe initial period of adjustment. These programs of "minimum employment" or "solidarity" also served as mechanisms for social control over the most marginal sectors of society and brought about changes in state institutions to implement social policies.

The ideological criticism of inefficiency in the welfare state and the failure of the subsidiary state gave way to the targeting of assistance to so-called vulnerable groups, as manifested in the proliferation of emergency funds promoted by international organizations.[103] Welfare programs and targeting (*focalización*), despite the significant accomplishments of the latter, generated a change in the orientation of the state and society toward the poor. Poor people were transformed from "actors" with regard to social policies, including mechanisms to process their demands sometimes with their participation, into "beneficiaries" of targeted policies.

Agencies responsible for targeting the poor are slowly replacing the state institutions that used to administer traditional social services in health, education, and housing. Examples include Progresa in Mexico and *bolsa escola* in Brazil, where direct payments to poor families are conditioned on children's school attendance and performance and the allowance goes to the female head of household rather than to the male. This tendency deflects attention from the need for an integral state reform, which over the long term would narrow the wide divergence in life chances among social groups. After initial savings are achieved, social policy targeting and fiscal austerity become a zero sum game, in which business sectors and the political right oppose increasing state expenditures or higher taxes. The state is caught in the paradox of accepting the responsibility for social improvements without the resources to do so, which arouses further criticism of state lethargy and inefficiency. In sum, no social policy (targeted or structural) can be effective if it does not re-endow the state with influence over national development and a real capacity to allocate resources.[104]

State reform is not simply a dogma to reduce its size and extension but needs to be an outcome of a decision regarding the desired functions and principles of state action. The solution is neither simply to add new departments or agencies without altering old structures, nor to affirm that the magic potion is to trim state size. The proper approach could be that certain areas, such as justice and redistribution, need more employees and resources, that is, an increase in state size. In other areas, by contrast, such as banking and especially the military, it would be suitable to reduce state size. Carefully focused police action with regard to potential terrorist threats may be necessary in a number of Latin American countries (Colombia is obviously a more complex situation), but for Latin America as a whole, poverty is the main threat to internal peace, and available state resources under an emergent SPM would need to be redirected in part from coercive to redistributive state functions.

The area of justice is crucial for defining the relations between those who are included and excluded and the definition of citizenship. The pervasive criticisms of judicial systems worldwide are that "justice favors the powerful," that common folk have no access to it, and that it is incapable of curbing corruption. In other government policy areas, reforms are mainly directed at modernization, a more flexible bureaucracy, decentralization, and personnel training. The state also needs to address some new areas with executive authority and others with regulatory authority. These challenges require new structures (environment, intellectual property); new norms (communication, technology of information); and the reconfiguring of existing agencies (culture, education) toward regulation, orientation, and evaluation rather than the implementation of new programs. For example, the National Security Plan proposed by the Fox administration in Mexico essentially discarded internal political challenges to the regime as the main security threat.[105] Instead, it substituted such concerns as domestic and international organized crime, terrorism, corruption, and environmental deterioration as major risks. Building on these concerns, the Plan called for significant reforms of national security institutions.

The question is no longer simply one of access to goods or services or their coverage. Even for the poor, the question also is, What are the qualities of service in education, health, and justice? A parallel issue is the degree of institutionalized citizen participation in central and decentralized government programs. In some areas of state action, direct democracy (election of officials) is appropriate, while in others a reform of the state structure to permit noncorporatist representativeness near the point of delivery is needed. In all cases, effectiveness, efficiency, and responsiveness combined with accountability and transparency are essential.

In sum, if in the statist-national-popular matrix the state was the principal agent of development and social integration and also served as the principal referent for collective action, the successive reforms associated with the intent of imposing a new neoliberal model of development have sought to reduce the role of the state and to convert it both into a mechanism to make the new model viable and into an agent fostering globalization. In the face of this effort, new tendencies have emerged that seek to give back to the state its directing, regulating, and protecting roles. What is at stake in ongoing state reforms in different countries is precisely the confrontation between these two visions. A future sociopolitical matrix will depend in great part on how this issue is resolved, to the extent that the democratic character of the regime does not become the central question.

The Political Party System

Successful "stateness" requires that actors in society believe, to one degree or another, that the state belongs to them. This identification is usually manifested by a mechanism of representation such as a party system. Yet, the region as a whole has been marked by extremely unstable party systems and high rates of electoral volatility, as parties and party systems have tended to move away from increased institutionalization and coherence. Historically, the Latin American region has experienced considerably more electoral volatility when compared to European democracies; this volatility grew from the 1980s into the 1990s, though with considerable cross-national variation. Congruent with our matrix framework, there is evidence that various explanations put forward to explain this may be relevant. These include economic factors, such as sharply fluctuating growth and inflation rates; institutional factors relating particularly to the age of parties, but also to discontinuities in electoral rules or patterns; and, to a lesser extent, social-structural factors relating to declines in union density.[106] The countries with seemingly the most stable or oldest party systems within the region, Colombia, Honduras, and Uruguay, are also marked in the first two cases by the strength of oligarchic continuities. Likewise, in these three countries, as in most Latin American countries, clientelistic practices have proved extremely resilient. In turn, party systems built around labor mobilization have experienced far more party erosion, volatility, and/or programmatic change.[107]

The central issue today concerning political parties, however, is not simplistically their continuity but, more fundamentally, society's capacity to build strong party systems that are able to re-establish links with an increasingly fragmented and often disappointed society, delivering demands and support and responding to grievances of a nearly dismantled state. It is apparent that the crises of the region's party systems and of political representation have continued into the current decade, although precise challenges and responses to them have varied among countries. In some, the crucial problem is the construction of solid parties that meet the minimum criteria of what a party is in terms of representation, appeal, and project and its capacity to govern, to oppose, and to make alliances. In countries where proper parties really do not exist, it is very probable that issues and social groups will not have representation at all. Alternatively, they will be appropriated and spuriously represented by personalities with political ambitions coming from the media, the entertainment industry, sports, the military, or some other "anti-party" constituency or by particularistic lobbies with social influence. The Peruvian, Ecuadorian, and Venezuelan cases particularly illustrate the need for the creation of viable parties.[108]

In other countries, parties as such exist, but the challenge of consolidating a party system able to represent the entire ideological spectrum or the different social sectors still persists. Yet, there are significant contrasts. In some cases, multiparty systems appear to be emerging, although from very different starting points. For example, in Uruguay, the traditional dichotomy between the National Party (Partido Nacional) and the Colorado Party (Partido Colorado) has been replaced by a three-party scheme with the presence of a broad leftist coalition, the Broad Front (Frente Amplio — FA), as a force capable of winning national level elections. And, in Mexico, the historical one-party hegemony of the PRI has been effectively overcome with the conformation of a multiparty system that includes the National Action Party (Partido de Acción Nacional — PAN) and the Party of the Democratic Revolution (Partido de la Revolución Democrática — PRD). This dramatic political mutation led to the first defeat of the PRI in a presidential election, when Vicente Fox assumed the presidency in 2000. In contrast, in Argentina and Paraguay, after periods suggesting the successful emergence of multiparty systems, the countries would now appear to be returning to situations of virtual one-party dominance. In Argentina, this is a result of the return of Peronism (Peronist Party/Partido Justicialista) to power after the collapse of the government of the Alliance (Alianza) coalition, with the resignation of President de la Rúa at the end of 2001 and the effective liquidation of the parties that supported his government, the Radical Civic Union (Unión Cívica Radical — UCR) and Front for the Country in Solidarity (Frente del País Solidario — FREPASO). And in Paraguay, party politics appear reduced to the sometimes turbulent competition across different factions of the Colorado Party. Another situation applies where parties and the party system are consolidated both in the sense that there are not new parties and that parties interact, but the problem is the rebuilding of linkages with society, constituencies, and public opinion. This seems to be the case in Chile.

Party system institutionalization itself is not static, as the collapse of the Democratic Action (Acción Democrática — AD) and the Committee of Independent Electoral Political Organization (Comité de Organización Política Electoral Independiente — COPEI) and the emergence of the Chavista movement in Venezuela have demonstrated in a particularly dramatic fashion. It responds to economic change, new social movements, institutional features, and the links of parties to groups in society. Over this past decade, there has been a veritable transformation of how individual citizens and social groups perceive and link up with political leaders, challenging the basic idea of a political party. Some of these changes hark back to themes of political populism and movementism (*movimientismo*). Others, in turn, mirror attitudes in the wealthier democracies, such as a decline in the people's trust of government. The discrediting of the legislature, the judiciary, or the executive is not unique to Latin America. Nor is it a consequence of a diffusion effect of dissatisfaction from north to south. Rather, similar, more severe economic and social dislocations appear to have led to corresponding phenomena across regions, though available data suggest they occur in a more intensified fashion in Latin America.[109]

To conclude, we can underscore two positive tendencies that, at the same time, pose dilemmas and risks of their own. One is that during the 1990s, some party systems have successfully confronted the risk of immobilism under presidentialism by establishing relatively stable governing coalitions: among these are the examples of Uruguay; Bolivia, especially around the Nationalist Revolutionary Movement (Movimiento Nacionalista Revolucionario — MNR); Brazil (under the two presidential periods of Cardoso); and, especially, Chile, with the center-left Concertation (Concertación) of the Christian Democratic Party (Partido Demócrata Cristiano — PDC), the Radical Party (Partido Radical — PR), the Party for Democracy (Partido por la Democracia — PPD), and the Socialist Party (Partido Socialista — PS). In Chile, the Concertación successfully transformed itself from a grouping of parties promoting the end of authoritarianism into an extraordinarily stable governing coalition; three presidents, including Ricardo Lagos, the first socialist since the 1973 coup, have governed from 1990 to the present.

Brazil underscores a second positive tendency. In Brazil, there has been a process of party consolidation that has generated, as Rachel Meneguello argues, a "virtuous" cycle across representation, electoral performance, and governing. This virtuous cycle has included feedback from the positive impact of the participation of the political parties in government to their electoral performance. Under the two Cardoso administrations, there were two principal areas of consolidation. One was with regard to party participation in Congress, which permitted parties to gain cabinet representation. Governing parties defined "party territories" within the state, that is, mechanisms of party control over sectoral ministries and resources that lasted across presidential terms. These areas of articulation influenced the second key area of consolidation, namely, the progressive internal institutionalization of the parties.[110] The triumph of President Lula da Silva of the Workers Party (Partido dos Trabalhadores — PT) in the 2002 presidential elections opens up the possibility of the full integration of Brazil's party system. This party system was practically divided into two camps, one consisting of the heirs of the parties created by the military during Brazil's most recent authoritarian period and its multiple divisions, and the other by the PT, which, in spite of having attained posts at the state and municipal levels, had not fully abandoned some anti-system demands until Lula's 2002 victory.

At the same time, these two tendencies present risks. Government coalitions have often, in fact, been quite fragile, as was demonstrated in Bolivia and Uruguay in 2000. At the same time, the Latin American experience, including that of Brazil, also demonstrates that it is not desirable that political parties become transformed simply into managers of the *res publica* (public concerns), abandoning or declaring as irrelevant any representational, identity-based or ideological link to their electorates. In a context in which the various political parties define themselves equally as ideologically pragmatic, and, in fact, all share a similar economic outlook, there is a risk at the extreme that the parties will end up representing nobody except themselves in their quest for position and influence.

Ideology and Political Parties

Historically, the extent to which ideology permeated party politics varied considerably across Latin America, though throughout the region this now appears to be in decline.[111] In Chile, social polarization was clearly expressed through the party system, and in Argentina there was a strong overlap between class and party affiliation. The Broad Front, appearing in Uruguay in the 1970s, transformed what had been a two-party system with a predominant party into a two-and-one-half or three-party system. However, as noted, Uruguay, Colombia, and Honduras have been marked for much of their modern histories by nonideological parties, based on strong levels of inherited party identification, preventing them from becoming simply "catch-all" electoral machines. Peru, first with APRA and then with the more ephemeral rise of the United Left (Izquierda Unida — IU), also experienced ideological party politics with a degree of popular electoral support, even if the final result was the pulverization of the parties, particularly those on the left. And in Brazil, in the midst of profound party underdevelopment and a highly fragmented party system, the PT emerged as an authentic class-based party, gradually moderating over time as it retained organizational coherence. In other countries that experienced a degree of democratic experience, such as Costa Rica and Venezuela, predominant parties with important ties to labor, respectively, the National Liberation Party (Partido de Liberación Nacional — PLN) and Democratic Action, functioned within a two-party system until the late 1990s. The increasingly overlapping programmatic orientations of the parties in the absence of hereditary party identifications helped make them more similar to the European "catch-all" parties. All of these countries have also been marked to a greater or lesser extent by clientelistic relationships, exchanging particularistic benefits for votes.

Ideological or ideologized parties directed their electoral appeals and mobilizational efforts toward social groups with their own organizations and auxiliary associations. These unions, professional and cultural associations, and peasant leagues, in turn, have often played a central role in the organization of interests in civil society, with the clearest Latin American case being Chile. In general, where parties consolidated themselves as electoral organizations with congressional representation prior to the development of a strong state or of well-organized societal interests (as in Colombia, Chile, and Uruguay), the parties tended to become powerful intermediaries between civil society and the state; in turn, where strong state institutions preceded party development, as in Brazil, the parties typically did not assume such a role.

In an emerging SPM, an effective party system appears to require parties that reach out to broad sectors of the population with a mix of approaches. In Latin America's historical experience, parties that relied purely on ideological or programmatic appeals sometimes encouraged excessive sectarianism in and polarization of society. In turn, those that relied almost exclusively on clientelism or specific material benefits sometimes ultimately bred excessive corruption and cynicism about the political process, encouraging many to retreat into apathy or employ means outside of electoral channels to express their political demands. During the Allende years, Chilean political parties approximated the former; in the last several decades, the traditional Colombian parties have approached the latter.

The decline of the ideological content of party programs and group-based mobilizational efforts by party machines has been occurring for several reasons. Socialist or populist parties, such as the AD in Venezuela, the Peronists in Argentina, and the Socialists in Chile, embraced, with some variations, free market economics. Other parties, like Mexico's PRI, reluctantly accepted neoliberal economics as a fait accompli and struggled to reconcile it with old party slogans and platforms. The disjuncture between campaign promises and austerity policies, in the context of continuing fiscal crises, generated a far sharper divergence between what the government said and what it did than was previously the case. At another level, there is reason to believe that the turn to more market-oriented policies and a reduction in the state's role in the economy has eroded both clientelistic and ideological (in terms of socialist or populist welfare programs) capabilities of political parties and strengthened other forms of clientelism not directly linked to parties.

We are witnessing a move in Latin America from global ideological politics to approaches, sometimes programmatic, of a more limited scope. This seems to be part of a worldwide phenomenon but is unlike the re-emergence of virulent nationalism in the Baltic states, the vigor of Islamic fundamentalism, or even the limited expressions of millenarianism in the region, such as Peru's Shining Path. The decline of globally ideological politics is not likely to be replaced by stable or coherent religious, national, ethnic, or identity-based mobilization.

Admittedly, in countries that previously experienced bitter polarization — notably Chile — a greater reliance on the instruments of politics may be viewed as positive. Yet, even countries that had not had particularly ideological politics still often had highly divisive politics, as the stakes for "ins" and "outs" regarding control of the state, especially in winner-take-all presidential systems, remained high (witness the civil wars in Costa Rica and Colombia). However, as noted earlier, the de-ideologizing of politics may actually be a symptom of party system decline and of further movement toward personalism and clientelism, rather than of institutional "maturation."

A consequence of politics, viewed almost exclusively in instrumental terms as a struggle for control over a limited state and power resources, may well move beyond depolarization to depoliticization, apathy, resignation, and withdrawal from party politics. Evidence indicates this is occurring in countries moving more toward "normalization," such as Chile, and in those marked by "personalization," such as Argentina. In countries with recent transitions to democratic rule, this has not meant a rejection of democratic practices in the short term, though over time disgruntlement is growing. And, public discontent with politicians and parties can be manipulated for or supportive of antidemocratic actions, as in Fujimori in Peru and the *bolivarianos* in Venezuela.

In sum, if sectarianism and polarization can be considered the dark side of ideological politics in the previous era, cynicism, corruption, and episodic mobilization of rage could increasingly become the dark side of contemporary, pragmatic, instrumental politics.

Communications and Corruption

Any future SPM must resolve issues relating to the quality of politics in a situation defined both by globalization and trivialization. Some crucial issues that formerly relied exclusively on politics (for example, property, which was part of all leftist party projects) tend to have disappeared from the political agenda. Instead, new issues coming from society demand to be taken into account by political actors who frequently are unable to respond to them effectively. Analytically, this can also be presented as the fact that political parties and party systems, founded around different cleavages and projects, are increasingly challenged to accommodate the emerging new cleavages and projects.

It is increasingly less possible for power holders in the region, whether public or private, to insulate the populace from important world trends, especially as Latin America is so effectively integrated into the dominant U.S. networks. This fact, true to a greater or lesser extent for economic elites in Latin America, is now also true for broader sectors of the population, with their access to television, and to middle-sector groups, who routinely travel abroad, use computers and e-mail, and communicate via modems and fax machines. Rapid communication has profound effects on the policy-making process of states, as political leaders, bureaucrats, and social actors all seek support, information, and resources from abroad in promoting their positions.

Domestically, one of the most significant political effects of the communications revolution is in the management of electoral campaigns. The complexity, sophistication, and cost of campaigns have all increased dramatically. The media, particularly television, are paid partners in projects ranging from propagating ideological and often group-based appeals to image manipulation and persuasion packages for individuals across social strata. For example, it is ironic that Chile, a country that appears to be a paradigm of an organized party system, altogether lacks a law regulating campaigns and parties' finances.

The role of money in politics and political corruption are related questions. Any intelligent discussion of the changing role of corruption in Latin American politics is hampered by one major problem: there are no accurate measurements of its dimensions, and it is difficult to state with assurance that, in fact, there is more or less corruption now than in previous decades. Lack of trust in the legislature and in the judiciary is closely linked to issues of corruption in most Latin American countries. At the same time, there are several reasons to believe that even in countries where there may well be less corruption now, the political tolerance for corruption is also much lower. The political impact of accusations of corruption is greater now on a continent-wide basis than in previous periods, as is evident in the cases of Collor de Mello in Brazil, Carlos Andrés Pérez in Venezuela, Serrano in Guatemala, Menem in Argentina, and Fujimori in Peru.

Corruption is commonly understood as an appropriation of public goods for illicit private gain.[112] Corruption usually has been associated with a large state, particularly state enterprises and agencies involved in procurement, and with the enforcement of extensive and complex regulatory practices. Within the region, Mexico was an extreme example of this. Theoretically, after a state rids itself of state-run enterprises and deregulates, corrupt practices should be minimized. However, the processes of deregulation (who receives information and when) and particularly privatization of state assets (who is sold what and at what price) have been especially amenable to corrupt practices, depending upon how they were carried out. Privatization experiences in Chile under Pinochet, Argentina under Menem, and Mexico under Salinas are examples of this type of corruption. Theoretically, countries that have already deregulated and sold off state enterprises should have reduced opportunities for corruption relative to what existed before, but this has not been confirmed so far in countries where corruption was prevalent in periods prior to the privatizations. Furthermore, the case of Fujimori in Peru has highlighted how extensively issues of corruption, in the pursuit of wealth and efforts to retain state power, can retain relevancy even following privatization.

Yet, there is another dimension that is widely viewed as corruption: practices of clientelism, nepotism, and favoritism inherent to some extent in all political party practices throughout the world. The dislike of politicians and a disdain of politics as corrupt are as evident in weak, fragmented, multiparty systems like Brazil's as in stronger party systems, such as those of pre-1998 Venezuela. Effective participation in party affairs and genuine responsiveness by party leaders with some degree of accountability, even if not fully programmatic, appear largely absent in both cases. In contrast, the political class in Chile has not been challenged widely by accusations of corruption, and its party system, even when the parties are criticized, remains legitimate, based on public opinion polls, particularly in a comparative regional context. However, only a detailed, country by country analysis, considering both the state and the party dimensions, could fully determine whether corruption over this recent period of democratization and neoliberal economic reforms has actually increased or decreased.

What is clear is that the political impact of corruption's perceived existence has increased. The increased political impact of corruption cannot be reduced to a single factor. Explanations typically begin with the continent's democratizing context in a post-Cold War era and then consider such issues as the rise of new political figures to power, some of whom based their electoral campaigns on promises of honesty, for example, Collor de Mello in Brazil and Salvador Jorge Blanco in the Dominican Republic. Other explanations for increased attention to corruption are the fiscal crisis of the state, the nature of privatization, the impact of economic crisis on middle sector groups, a more independent role for the media, assistance to emerging watchdog citizen groups in various countries from transnational networks, and the growing expenses of electoral campaigns. In some cases, the hubris of power in contexts of extreme personalization of presidential privilege may have led key figures to perceive they had an invulnerability that in the end they did not possess.

In periods of dramatic policy shifts, access to power becomes especially important to conglomerates and other businesses, especially those that provide goods or services to the state or hope to acquire them from the state. The corrupt and semi-corrupt linkages across the politically powerful and the economically wealthy often become more visible when new groups or figures come to power. The "rules" for access may change somewhat, as may some of the players allowed to participate. Complaints are voiced, somewhat hypocritically, by those previously "in" who now find themselves "out" or as a consequence of the less sophisticated fashion in which the exchanges of access for money occur.

This process at the "top" may be reinforced by what occurs at the "bottom." Particularly in countries that continue to be affected by a serious fiscal crisis of the state, the pay scales of public employees have declined considerably. Thus, many more public sector employees have been forced to seek additional jobs, and some may accept bribes to augment their incomes. This "low-level" corruption can help create the perception of a generalized atmosphere of corruption. Middle-sector groups whose standard of living has been most negatively affected by economic crisis tend to focus particularly on corruption and impunity issues, especially in a context of more generalized crime and an inoperative criminal justice system. However, the extent to which corruption will be pursued remains a function of the political power of the actors involved. For example, while in power, President Salinas and his relatives were immune to any suggestions of impropriety. Out of power, they were in exile or in jail. Collor de Mello of Brazil, unlike Ernesto Samper in Colombia, was vulnerable to impeachment on corruption charges, in part because of his relative political isolation, reflected in the fact that he was not at the head of a party that held a majority in his national Congress. Menem of Argentina and Fujimori of Peru were not pursued by judicial authorities until they vacated the presidential palace. In Chile, the Congress was not allowed to investigate corruption under the Pinochet regime, and the Frei administration did not pursue a corruption case involving checking accounts that affected the Pinochet family.

The mass media generate two contradictory effects.[113] On the one hand, the media limit states' ability to cut off the citizenry from ideas or events occurring abroad and even within their own countries. On the other hand, in conjunction with public opinion polling, they may also serve as a powerful new tool of manipulation. Targeted media efforts and real or orchestrated band-wagon effects can mobilize votes of the growing numbers of "unorganized poor."

The mass media have also played a central role in some cases, such as in Brazil and Venezuela, by highlighting incidences of corruption and the apparent impunity of the central actors involved. As the media in Latin America have become less dependent on the state yet more dependent on ratings linked to sensationalist issues, they have tended to focus more attention on the issue of public corruption, thus at times shifting attention away from corruption's private sector links. Paradoxically, the growing importance of the mass media has also been a central factor in the increased cost of electoral campaigns. Indeed, many politicians allege their corrupt practices are linked to campaign activities rather than goals of personal enrichment (the two, of course, are not mutually exclusive). Vast sums of money raised in largely unregulated fashion help denigrate the democratic process, and, as in Colombia under Samper, there is always the question of what the money has bought. Peru under Fujimori provides a particularly dramatic example of how personalized presidential power in the absence of effective legislative and judicial checks leaves the door open for corrupt practices.

Heightened awareness of corruption under these circumstances will not necessarily lead to a decrease in corruption, although it will spur moralizing rhetoric and occasionally make scapegoats of previously powerful personalities. So, there are contradictory trends at work in the region. Deregulation and privatization may limit certain opportunities for corruption while creating others. However, corruption involves not only the public sector but also the private sector. If the state does not generate adequate oversight and regulatory capabilities, corruption may simply be replaced by predatory oligopolistic or oligopsonistic practices to the benefit of concentrated conglomerates or individuals in the private sector (not to ignore securities fraud visited upon unsuspecting investors). If the case of the ignominious collapse of Enron in 2002 demonstrates the power of money to gain political access to help assure excessively lax regulation in the United States, other examples abound in the region and throughout the world of how free market, small state economies provide opportunities for private actors and corporations to corrupt officials and politicians through campaign finance, lobbying for favorable legislation, and selective tax collection.

It remains to be seen whether corrupt habits persevere in Latin America in a new SPM or whether concerned citizens, parties, and a press independent from state and private interests can curb corruption through increased cooperation with judicial authorities, even as old patterns decline and potential opportunities diminish. In the most optimistic scenario, an enraged citizenry demands higher civic virtue from its leaders, loudly voicing its democratic preferences. Although there are signs of this phenomenon, the structural bases for corruption remain substantial.

Governability

A last question concerning the transformation of the state, parties, and politics refers to governability.[114] Our vision permits a significant modification and broadening of the conventional meaning of the concept of governability. The term's origins could be perceived as reactionary, to the extent that they were prompted by the explosion of social demands and suggested as a response to the reduction of the state, its atomization, and, at the limits, repression as ways to deprive social actors of their instruments of pressure. Today governability does not refer to an abstract principle but to a specific regime, that is, democratic governability. It does not involve reducing the state or diminishing its ability to represent demands by political parties in order to suffocate incipient demands, atomize potentially disruptive actors, or restrict democratic mechanisms. Rather, the opposite, governability can be viewed as the strengthening of the leadership capacity of the state, the representativeness of political parties, the autonomy and empowerment of social actors, and the deepening of democratic institutions. In other words, governability understood in this way is a normatively charged concept, involving the establishment or the recomposition of a sociopolitical matrix with these relevant characteristics at a high level of quality. In contrast, the cases of a "voiding of politics" in some countries of Latin America — where the citizenry abdicates decisionmaking to political leaders who they may occasionally ratify in power via elections only to retreat into apathy, generalized depoliticization around central public issues, or consumerism — run counter to our sense of governability.

THE SOCIOCULTURAL DIMENSION

The decomposition of the statist-national-popular SPM implied profound changes for social actors, social movements, and the sociocultural model.[115] Under military dictatorships, social action was imbued with interwoven meanings. The first challenge was to reconstruct the social fabric destroyed during the period of authoritarianism and economic reform. The second was the politicization of all demands so that the purpose of every action was the end of the authoritarian regime. Social movements' relationship with politics and the state changed dramatically, as groups became more autonomous, symbolic, and oriented toward asserting their own identities in place of instrumental or material demands. The evolution of collective action during these regimes can be viewed first as self defense and survival, followed by opposition to military-dictated procedures and a call for a return to democracy, and finally as insisting on a political role in the transition.

The challenge to the constitutional and legalistic bases of military power fortified the autonomy and self-confidence of social groups. This process gave rise to a "resurrection of civil society" and a debate around "new social movements."[116] In some cases, these expressions of civil society were put on the defensive by the new economic model, which eroded positions that had been won under the statist-national-popular SPM. In other cases, the mobilization of these groups reached their peak when the authoritarian systems smothered normal forms of political expression, and the groups broke ties with the party system as they articulated new themes in the public agenda, such as gender; religious, ethnic, or regional identity; ecological questions; urban safety; and issues related to the informal economy. But these changes, dramatic and significant as they are, did not lead these actors to become much more autonomous or stable and certainly did not universalize a system of representation in the post-authoritarian period.

As detailed in earlier sections, structural transformations combined with the ideological power of neoliberalism were at least as crucial as the more purely repressive acts of authoritarian regimes in disarticulating the statist-national-popular SPM. Beyond the authoritarian regimes' repressive capabilities, their ability to discard the previous sociocultural model also affected the collectivist, statist, and politicized orientations of the middle class and popular sectors. These regimes increasingly replaced these orientations with a neoliberal ideology that emphasized individualism not only as a strategy to deal with the market but as a paradigm of society overall. Neoliberal ideology also stressed societal self-regulation and decentralization as substitutes for political representation.[117]

The transformations associated with the disarticulation of the previous sociopolitical matrix have brought about significant changes in the nature of the actors and the social movements in Latin America and in the region's sociocultural model. Evidently, a new SPM will imply a wider distance between politics and economics. What is more apparent is the rupture of the old model, yet new forms of sociopolitical control and regulation over the market are still missing.

There are reasons to believe that a new central Social Movement will not emerge to give meaning to the multiple social movements that operate currently in Latin American countries. As noted, a national-popular Social Movement was important in the previous SPM, and the struggles for democratic transition created a democratic Social Movement. However, in most countries following democratic transitions, political actors and processes were central to the social action efforts to preclude authoritarian regression, even as the focus on economic stability privileged the requirements of economic restructuring, also discouraging collective action, which could challenge its realization.

Currently, at least three problems continue to militate against the emergence of a new central Social Movement. First, poverty has increased, and these societies are experiencing a new type of exclusion. A contradiction exists between those who operate "inside" the socioeconomic and political systems, irrespective of their relative position on the interior, and those categories, actors, or movements who are "outside." While the latter may penetrate the systems in differing degrees, this gap between the insiders and outsiders makes organized collective action very difficult. Also, the model of modernity is questioned not only by groups on the margin, but also by those who participate within the system but at a subordinate level.

Women, the young, indigenous groups, and especially the poor are examples of categories that are penetrated by the "in-out" contradictions, even if in cultural terms they are integrated through the communications media. Those outside the system, concentrated among sectors of the peasantry, indigenous groups, and the urban poor, are seen by many insiders as unnecessary and superfluous. At this time, there are no important ideological currents or political organizations, as there were during the 1970s, that purposely take these people into consideration.

Second, the construction of new relations between the state and society creates new difficulties for the appearance of a central Social Movement. The old matrix had the characteristic of fusing different problems and dimensions of the society, facilitating a central Social Movement. A new matrix, in turn, would need to accommodate its differentiated components with more autonomy, tension, and interaction among them. The role of politics will be different, as will be the roles of the state, the party systems, and the popular movements. Each sphere of society will separate itself and, with its own contradictions, give rise to heterogeneous collective action with few common principles. Therefore, at the same time as diversity and social identities proliferate, the symbolic and organic links that might unify them in a central SM will also become weaker.

Third, beyond democratic consolidation and transitions, other changes are going to influence the characteristics of a central SM and its component social movements. In the statist-national-popular SPM, the struggles and conflicts were principally oriented toward collectivist, egalitarian, and national principles. The diverse tendencies and movements that were anticapitalist, antioligarchic, democratic, anti-imperialist, and nationalistic were most likely to adopt these principles. As mentioned earlier, in the statist-national-popular SPM, politics was the principal sphere of social action. These struggles and principles persist without being satisfied and still continue to stimulate scattered collective actions, but each one of the principles has become more technical, autonomous, and complex. Thus, the old forms of organization like labor unions, parties, or corporatism tend to be inadequate.

Changes in civil society have brought new types of demands that cannot express themselves through the old struggles for equality, liberty, and national sovereignty. In addition to the environment and regional autonomy, these include the collective rights of ethnic groups and new areas in daily life that have emerged relating to the model of modernity now in play. These areas include interpersonal and intergenerational relations; individual and group aspirations for social recognition, belonging, and identity; and demands for freedom from fear of threats to personal security. These demands pertain more to the dimension of seeking happiness, personal fulfillment, or a better quality of life, and they cannot be replaced or represented by the old mechanisms of collective action (unions and parties). These are not simply personal concerns, as the demands express themselves in the public sphere. Nor are they a pure expression of individualism, as might be expressed in new norms of consumerism, because they are also being pressed as a demand of "ours" and not just of "mine." What is important is that a policy that ignores the felt needs of subjects cannot address these social demands. Thus, they relate both to modernity and to the search for a new SPM. The demands for goods and services of the modern society, now extended to symbolic or cultural services, no longer are just simple demands for access to them, as they are determined by the diversity of each subject's needs and aspirations. And, quality of service becomes a requisite of equity at a higher level.

At the same time, with regard to issues that were classically in the domain of the nation-state under the previous SPM, there are emergent efforts to seek out new forms of global connections across international and domestic NGOs and social movements and new dialogues and confrontations with transnational corporations concerning issues such as labor rights, product quality, and the environment. It is still far too early to tell how much of an impact these movements will have. What is clear is that they represent another indication of the disappearance of the model of the former SPM, which had a more significant role for the national state and for politics as a dominant sphere of action.[118]

Latin America is experiencing a growing diversity in society, not limited to one sphere such as economics or politics. During the statist-national-popular SPM, politics was the principal channel of integration; the state allocated differential access to goods and services and endowed individual and collective life with meaning through ideological projects. Today, politics is just one of these channels, and "culture" — understood as the search for meanings and the coming together of symbolic representations, values, and lifestyles — acquires its own consistency and density. This new pattern manifests itself in the demands of indigenous people, regional and women's movements, the divergent lifestyles of the youth, the material and symbolic consumption patterns of the middle class, changes in the family unit, and new social relations. These realms become theaters of subjectivity and debates, frequently heated, over diverse ways of living one's life. At the same time, the various conventional areas of culture — called science, arts, ethnicity, education, communication, and cultural heritage — have each acquired their own autonomy and dynamism. "Culture" no longer is a reflection of politics and indeed starts dictating the content of politics. Each of these realms produces its own conflicts and social actors, who dispute and defend their individual and collective interpretations of aesthetics, truth, and goodness. Political struggles are increasingly disputes over society's cultural model.[119] However, this new meaning of politics is obscured, and even hidden by the situations of crisis in which all struggles appear linked to the defense of interests and material needs. And, it is also obscured by some resistance of politicians to accept this new meaning, as they seek to sustain "business as usual." Thus, their activity tends to be self-referential, a situation that cannot be resolved by trying to reduce politics into the resolution of "people's problems," as is asserted simplistically by some who criticize traditional political-ideological activity.

What is foreseen in the near future is a variety of forms of mobilization, which will be more autonomous, short-term, and less guided by politicians. Political struggles will be channeled more through institutions than through protest, and more oriented toward sectoral demands, partial modernizations, gradual democratization, and social integration and less toward radical global change. The content of political conflict will be divided between demands for inclusion and a search for meaning and specific identity in the face of the universalization of modernity as proposed by market forces and their agents. However, in situations of socioeconomic crisis, it is very probable that the forms of sectoral collective action will escape from institutional frameworks rejecting all official political actors; at the same time, they will do so demanding the presence of the state, though without much confidence or hope in it, while also presenting opposing principles of citizenship and self-determination. The alternative to this does not appear to be the revolutionary movements of the past but a retreat into apathy or communitarian reclusiveness.[120] In any event, what is no longer present is the absorption of social diversity by means of official political activity. This does not mean the end of politics, as some have indicated, nor a reduction of its scope simply to the provision of solutions to people's immediate problems, as neoliberalism and neopopulism indicate; rather, it means a change in the function and meaning of politics. More than serving as the means to goods offered by the state or the only source of meaning for collective life, as in the previous SPM, politics will have to become the central dimension that assures the existence of the state and national polity in a globalized world with fragmented societies.

Chapter Six

A NEW SOCIOPOLITICAL MATRIX?

In the previous chapters, we have discussed several critical political, economic, social, and cultural changes that have affected Latin America in the context of a globalizing world. These changes and this context have redefined the model of modernization away from one derived from industrial society, based on the dynamic interaction of major social actors in which the state has a central mobilizing role. As a consequence, the very concept of development has been reformulated. Development now can be understood as centered around four processes, none of which can be reduced to or explained by any of the others:

1. The construction of political democracies;
2. Social democratization, including national integration;
3. The reinsertion of the Latin American economies into the world system; and
4. The building of a model of modernity that assumes both globalization and cultural identities.

The concept of sociopolitical matrix, understood as the relationships among the state, the political system of representation, the socioeconomic base of social actors, and cultural relations — mediated by the political regime — provides a means to place these complex phenomena into a comprehensive analytical framework, within which more specific arguments can be advanced.

Like other historical events, the emergence of a new sociopolitical matrix is subject to the "historical Doppler effect," which, similar to acoustics, creates a more homogeneous (lower pitched) interpretation for distant eras and sharper, more complex (higher pitched) interpretations in periods closer to the present. Historical generalizations seem more valid for time frames that are well in the past. Differentiation is dull among analytical cases, beginning and ending dates, and supporting evidence and exceptions. The closer the historical phenomenon is to the present, the more it is defined by demonstrable facts, many of which are inconsistent with or ambiguous for the general trends. Thus, historians typically have greater difficulty generalizing about recent periods, measured in decades, than those separated by centuries or millennia. This historical Doppler effect affects interpretations of development models and the sociopolitical matrix; it also permits less reliable conclusions on the emerging new approach than the one being transcended.

The transition toward a new sociopolitical matrix is much broader than the movement from one type of political regime to another or from one economic model to another, as it entails a weaving together of a whole new set of links across the political, economic, social, and cultural spheres. Even though each of these spheres retains its own autonomy and dynamism and is not reducible one to the others, each one has mutual effects on the others, which must be analyzed by any specific analysis of a particular historical period and society. This leads us to believe that the processes and structures are of long maturation and duration. We can expect an extended period of transition, characterized by the four processes discussed above and countertendencies, which will define the new Latin American *problematique*.

A central argument we have advanced is that changes in each of the elements of the SPM and in how they have related to each other over the past decades have disarticulated what we call the statist-national-popular sociopolitical matrix. During the 1970s, the military dictatorships of Chile and Argentina launched early attempts to build a new market-driven matrix based on neoliberal principles in order to replace the disarticulated one. These attempts to build a neoliberal market-driven matrix gained new momentum and expanded to other countries of the region in the 1980s, when the impact of the debt crisis, including the pressures exerted by the creditors, forced Latin American countries to dismantle further the old matrix (key characteristics of the neoliberal market-driven matrix are presented in Table 2).

Thus, during the 1980s and 1990s, three parallel processes overlapped: the protracted disarticulation of the statist-national-popular matrix; the progressively stronger drives to build an alternative, neoliberal market-driven matrix; and the struggles to resist the imposition of the latter. One of the consequences of this overlap was the intensification of negative trends, such as social decomposition and growing inequality, the shattering of class identity, and depoliticization. As a result of these trends, many observers described the 1980s as Latin America's "lost decade." However, especially in the 1990s, these negative processes seemed to be compensated for by positive developments, such as economic growth, the taming of inflation, political maturation, social mobility, and the assertion of new identities. The apologists of the neoliberal market-driven matrix would argue that the outcome was a more than satisfactory balance, but the late 1990s and early 2000s — when the international economy experienced successive crises and the instability of capital flows became substantially more acute — clearly indicate its negative effects. Thus, this period has witnessed the coexistence of contrasting trends: the further disarticulation of the old statist-national-popular matrix, efforts to preserve and perpetuate it, the resilience of new elements, and the crippling of the process of construction of a market-driven matrix. Indeed, the neoliberal project to construct a market-driven matrix has aborted in Latin America.

Table 2. Sociopolitical Matrices: Neoliberal Market-Driven and Multicentered

Characteristics	Attempted in the 1980s and 1990s and Failed	Current Reality for a Number of Latin American Countries	Potential (Not Assured)
Sociopolitical Matrix	**Neoliberal Market-Driven**	**No Matrix, Marked by Decomposition and Drift**	**Multicentered**
Components: state, political system of representation, socio-economic base of social actors, cultural relations, mediated by political regime	Market allocation preferred mechanism for decisionmaking. Spheres separate. Minimal role for the state and sharply reduced range of activities addressed through the political regime.	Absence of a matrix with components effectively interacting.	Components autonomous, complementary, and mutually reinforceable. Power deconcentrated. Discernible compatibility across the state, the economy, and representational system, nurtured by diversity and cultural innovation.
Development Model	Ideological belief in market-driven processes and an open economy. Minimal state role in any socioeconomic processes. Transfer of power and resources from the state to private economic actors with little effective regulation or oversight. Focus on citizens as consumers.	Countries marked by near permanent crises inhibiting generation of development model. Absence of any overarching policy consensus regarding the elements of a feasible, coherent, and just development model. Disparate proposals based on sectoral, class-based, regional, or ideological interests, some marked by strong disillusion with market economics. Unable to combine widespread backing with international viability.	State-guided and market-accepting, with incentives for local saving and investment. Adequate growth to absorb labor entrants and social policy oriented to poverty reduction and improvements in income distribution.
International Economy	Free flow of financial resources, unregulated by national states. Emphasis on competitiveness, comparative advantage, and open markets for trade. Monitoring by multilateral institutions such as the International Monetary Fund (IMF) and the World Bank dominated by industrialized countries.	Domestic economy strongly impacted by international fluctuations, with little autonomy and limited negotiating power vis-à-vis multilateral institutions such as the IMF and the World Bank and transnational corporations. Marked by oscillating patterns of indiscriminate opening to world economy and sharp withdrawal of foreign capital.	Selective sector-by-sector integration, accommodating dominant world trend. Regional integration agreements consolidated. Sufficient economic diversification and fiscal prudence to withstand external shocks.

Table 2. Sociopolitical Matrices: Neoliberal Market-Driven and Multicentered — *continued*

Civil Society, Actors/Subjects	Accepted within confines of general market model, with economically dominant groups concentrating influence in society and over the state and polity and many previously organized social actors and movements weakened or destroyed. Toleration for variations in identities and lifestyles absorbable by consumer culture. Social movements and organizations partially replace functions of the state as it withdraws.	Civil society space occupied mainly by political and economic elites but broader civil society marked by fragmentation and even incoherence. Popular sectors struggling to organize and achieve a meaningful voice in national affairs, with occasional dramatic influence. Significant strand of social-participatory, anti-globalization, counter-hegemonic groups, questioning the state and the polity. High levels of impunity and citizen insecurity.	Movement toward stronger organization and marked by greater differentiation. More diverse identities with global connections. Fluid influence networks both domestically and globally. Diffuse but strengthening links between elites and rank-and-file.
Ideology, Cultural Orientation	Individualism and individual competition as a system of societal self-regulation under capitalism. Multiple loci for the generation of social meanings. Symbolic representations, values, and lifestyles not opposed to market ideology or consumer culture.	Lack of integrating ideology. Generalized absence of interest in ideology combined with competing value systems, as political elites sometimes appeal to racial or nationalistic icons. Strong cultural penetration from the outside.	Democratic, market-accepting in a context of state intervention and regulation, globally aware, identity-based, with space for both individual and collective action. Respect for local cultural expression. Self-asserting and integrative, with space for diversity.
Political System of Representation	Weakened — as authority is centralized in order to enact market reforms. Greater weight to economically powerful groups and open to neopopulist appeals. Tendency to marginalize it or to enhance only its managerial capacity, making as many decisions as possible through market allocation.	Formal democracies unconsolidated or consolidated but incomplete; many with authoritarian enclaves. Collapse of the representational system in some countries and, in others, growing challenges to the ability of parties and party systems to represent citizen demands and maintain institutional links between citizenry and the state effectively.	The party system with less centrality but still with a crucial role in articulating political, socioeconomic, and cultural interests, reaching out to broad segments of the population. Ability of organized social movements, ethnic movements, and regional and lifestyle identities to influence the polity. Deepening of democracy.
Concept of Modernity	Ideal society modeled on individualist-rationalist-technological trends in advanced industrialized countries (such as Canada and the United States).	Multiple conceptions of modernity coexist. Important shaping role of international influences and cultural media. No consensus or integrative unity.	Universal values of human rights combined with diverse identities and expressions. Combination of rationality, subjectivity, and historical memory in each society.

Table 2. Sociopolitical Matrices: Neoliberal Market-Driven and Multicentered — *continued*

Role of the State	Crucial role in implanting market reforms, followed by withdrawal to a desired minimal role, restricted primarily to security, macro-economic management, and poverty alleviation, eschewing any significant role in advancing social justice or improving income distribution.	Weak stateness. Inability of the state to engage with and respond to vast segments of the citizenry. Low transparency and accountability. Weak rule of law.	Stateness is reconstructed. State devises and implements effective means to generate sustained growth; address poverty; and counter legal, social, economic, and other exclusions. Successfully articulates multiethnic conceptions in pluriethnic societies. Gains access to the global arena, advances in regional integration schemes, and influences supranational institutions to help elevate autonomy, security, and well-being.
Vulnerabilities/Risks	Highly dependent on unpredictable international trade opening and resource flows. Imperfect implementation of economic model encourages new forms of corruption and rent-seeking. Increased poverty and inequality and growth in informal sector. Disarticulation in forms of representation and social actors. Difficulty in achieving ideological consensus or widespread legitimacy. Institutional inability to accommodate multiple identities. Broadly inappropriate for Latin American reality.	Inability to forge a coherent development model, recreate stateness, or establish effective tools to address legal and social gaps. Subordinate international role. Disparate identities as barrier to social action. Social fragmentation opens way for plebiscitarian and/or demagogic movements and further weakening of state and political institutions. Continued inability to generate sustained economic growth or relieve poverty and inequality.	Lengthy maturation process, creating the image of a lack of national direction. Risk of inability to forge a coherent development model and to reinforce it through ideology or motivating vision. Risk of inability to create and sustain effective mechanisms to address legal and social gaps, subordinate international role, and weak stateness. Disparate identities and social fragmentation may inhibit action for common purposes.

This failure points to decomposition and drift, the current reality for a number of Latin American countries, as one possible, more extended scenario. Under this scenario, a country indiscriminately opens, by choice or obligation, to a world economy whose agents penetrate, dissect, and even dismantle local commerce and production, profiting from inefficient economic relations. Civil society would either lose much of its coherence (if it once had it) or never gain coherence, as economic disruption breaks down social relationships such as the family, community, and workplace organization. This scenario would bring about national austerity measures that would debilitate state political institutions, particularly those agencies responsible for safeguarding welfare, and the state would lose legitimacy before an exasperated and disappointed populace. While elites would try to justify many private and public sector actions in the name of neoliberalism, these beliefs would not capture widespread adherence in the society at large and would prove to be poor guides for designing a viable growth and distribution model. Though multiple conceptions of modernity might coexist latently, none would be capable of challenging the values flowing in from abroad in the communications and cultural media. Citizen insecurity increases, and criminal and other forms of violence are met by impunity. The result is not a matrix with effectively interacting components, but a disjointed reality that seems to characterize the relations between the state and society in a large number of countries in the region at the turn of the century. The trend can be prolonged or be a transitional period prior to a decisive movement toward one or another modal SPM forms.

Whether the current disturbing trends will continue or whether countries in the region can advance toward an ethically desirable potential new SPM — itself, of course, only one option among several possible SPMs, but the one we choose to focus on — will be shaped by several critical options along different dimensions. One relates to the international economy. Latin American societies can continue to adjust to the rules of the international economy, paying social costs and seeking economic gains. The most advantageous position for countries in the region would be a substantive integration with the world economy, in which they retain some national control over the price of exports, the choice of markets, and the entry of foreign investment. This would require a reinforcement of the regulatory capacity of the state internally and externally, which does not seem feasible in the absence of the collective negotiating power of more deeply rooted subregional integration schemes like MERCOSUR.

At the other extreme, a national economy could be the simple supplier of raw materials or cheap labor, in a subordinate position in buyer-driven and producer-driven commodity chains, as well as fully vulnerable to capricious financial markets. If their internal markets are large or their disillusion with (or rejection of) capitalism is acute, they might try to resist or reverse processes of integration, especially if they calculate that costs of integration are high and the gains scant. Indeed, autarky might be a dream solution for some economic theorists, though hardly a viable alternative.

Second, civil society can move toward greater differentiation, stronger identities (ethnic, regional, gender, religious, and cultural), more persistent demands, and stronger organization to become a force weighing on economic and political elites. Alternatively, social differentiation can mean fragmentation, tenuous and vulnerable identities, voiceless demands, and endemic conflicts, with civil society dominated by business interests and generally incapable of exerting much influence on government. Culture can emerge from the society's own production of art, music, science, and definition of modernity or be imported practically intact from abroad or imposed by entrenched cultural elites.

Third, stateness implies the ability of the political institutions to engender consensus, forge unity, provide for orderly succession, and, in short, to claim legitimacy from society. The economic and political disruptions during the decline of the statist-national-popular SPM eroded stateness, and Latin American countries have strived to restore or recreate it in differing degrees. From a democratic perspective, the preferred situation is continuous improvement both to critical state institutions that can implement goals and to the system of representation to give all sectors (including women, the poor, ethnic groups, youth, new social movements, and minorities) a voice and vote in their future. The reinforcement of political parties, in some cases perhaps their re-foundation, seems unavoidable. In contrast, atavistic forms of corporatism, delegative or patrimonial democracy, neopopulism, or new types of *caudillismo* are less fortuitous, although still preferable to the authoritarian rule of earlier periods.

Fourth, a national ideology encapsulates society's shared interpretive framework for understanding a people's place in history. A country's ideology can be integrative and self-asserting with space for diversity, while avoiding xenophobia. However, competing value systems can split societies, or political leaders can appeal rhetorically to racial or nationalistic icons to bolster their hold on power. While the degree of international economic opening, civil society activism, and stateness can vary in strength in a new SPM, a matrix cannot endure without an integrating ideology or national project.

Today, the region confronts a vacuum left by the failure of the neoliberal project. It is marked by a tendency toward decomposition and drift and the absence of a clear SPM, with ethically less desirable tendencies across the dimensions noted above (see Table 2 for a summary of its key characteristics). One can also see some weak attempts toward — and the most unlikely scenario of — a return to the statist-national-popular matrix. Similarly, to differing degrees across the region, there is a grassroots tendency with a social-participatory vision that builds on an anti-globalization, counter-hegemonic discourse and actions, centered in NGOs and other groups in civil society that often have transnational links, if not support, and tends to question the state and the polity.

Beyond all these, as discussed in each of the sections of Chapter Five, it is also possible to see, here and there, in some countries more than others, important tendencies, not always parsimonious or encompassed in a single national project, that point to new kinds of relations between the state and society and to the possibility of reconstructing a sociopolitical matrix. And, combining elements of an empirical-predictive character with those of a normative-aspirational one, we could project an emerging *multicentered SPM* that would possess characteristics sharply in contrast with the previous statist-national-popular SPM, the neoliberal market-driven project, and the current situation. This new multicentered SPM would be shaped fundamentally by the nature of its linkages with the world economy and by the strengthening, autonomy, complementarity, and mutually reinforceable interactions among the state, the system of representation, and civil society (see summary in far right column of Table 2).

It is not yet possible to specify the concrete forms that the new relations between the state and society might take, though stateness will be reconstructed and civil society will be marked both by stronger organization and greater differentiation, with diverse identities reinforced by fluid domestic and global networks. Similarly, one can also imagine the SPM's possibilities for enhancing the voice of countries in the region in the globalized world, in part through enhanced economic and political integration of the region. What is relatively clear is that the new institutional framework will be formally democratic, even if the exact composition of this democracy is uncertain. We would expect the party system to continue to play a central role in articulating interests from society, with organized social movements able to influence the polity in a context of deepening democracy.

Our aim is not to chart or prescribe in any precise fashion the character- istics of this new sociopolitical matrix but to signal its possibility. If comparable to its predecessor, the new SPM will emerge gradually and exist most markedly in the larger countries of the region. Based on our interpretation of the region's contradictory trends over the past several decades, such an SPM would be marked by the autonomy, mutual strengthening, and complementarity of its components. Admittedly, because of the many countervailing factors and contradictory forces and tendencies discussed in the previous chapters, due to the general crisis of Latin American societies at the beginning of this new century, it will be difficult to construct a new multicentered SPM such as this one whose potential characteristics we have sketched. However, gradual construction of such a new SPM beneficial to the great majority of the Latin American people is possible and, above all, desirable. Our vision thus builds on empirical observation and contains value-laden assumptions of a normative nature. It embraces an aspiration that the results will be an improved quality of life and enhanced future prospects for Latin American societies.

NOTES

1. Some of the ideas presented here have been developed in Manuel Antonio Garretón, 1995, "Democracia, modernización, desarrollo: Hacia una nueva problemática en América Latina," in *Dimensiones actuales de la sociología*, eds. M.A. Garretón and O. Mella (Santiago, Chile: Bravo y Allende); as well as in Manuel A. Garretón, 1999, *Política y sociedad entre dos épocas. América Latina en el cambio de siglo* (Buenos Aires: Homo Sapiens); Manuel Antonio Garretón, 2000, *La sociedad en que vivi(re)mos. Introducción sociológica al cambio de siglo* (Santiago: LOM Ediciones); and Manuel Antonio Garretón, 2002, "The New Sociopolitical Matrix," in *(Re)constructing Political Society*, eds. M.A. Garretón and E. Newman (Tokyo: United Nations University Press).

2. For a number of valuable examples, see Ruth Berins Collier and David Collier, 1991, *Shaping the Political Arena: Critical Junctures, the Labor Movement, and Regime Dynamics in Latin America* (Princeton, N.J.: Princeton University Press); Peter H. Smith, 1991, "Crisis and Democracy in Latin America," *World Politics* 43 (4); Peter H. Smith, ed., 1993, *The Challenge of Integration: Europe and the Americas* (Coral Gables, Fla.: North-South Center Press at the University of Miami); William C. Smith, Carlos H. Acuña, and Eduardo A. Gamarra, eds., 1994b, *Latin American Political Economy in the Age of Neoliberal Reform: Theoretical and Comparative Perspectives for the 1990s* (Coral Gables, Fla.: North-South Center Press at the University of Miami), and the companion book by the same editors (1994a), *Democracy, Markets, and Structural Reform in Latin America: Argentina, Bolivia, Brazil, Chile, and Mexico* (Coral Gables, Fla.: North-South Center Press at the University of Miami); Felipe Agüero and Jeffrey Stark, eds., 1998, *Fault Lines of Democracy in Post-Transition Latin America* (Coral Gables, Fla.: North-South Center Press at the University of Miami); Philip Oxhorn and Pamela K. Starr, eds., 1998, *Markets and Democracy in Latin America: Conflict or Convergence?* (Boulder, Colo.: Lynne Rienner Publishers); José Luis Reyna, ed., 1995, *América Latina a fines de siglo* (México D.F.: Fondo de Cultura Económica); and Peter H. Smith, ed., 1995, *Latin America in Comparative Perspective: New Approaches to Methods and Analysis* (Boulder, Colo.: Westview Press). An example of a global analysis of what could be called a Latin American political model is Alain Touraine, 1989, *América Latina: Política y Sociedad* (Madrid: Espasa Calpe).

3. See Evelyne Huber and Michelle Dion, 2002, "Revolution or Contribution? Rational Choice Approaches in the Study of Latin American Politics," *Latin American Politics and Society* 44: 3 (Fall): 1-28; Gerardo Munck, 2001, "Game Theory and Comparative Politics," *World Politics* 53 (2): 173-204; and Kurt Weyland, 2002, "Limitations or Rational-Choice Institutionalism for the Study of

Latin American Politics," *Studies in Comparative International Development* 37: 1 (Spring): 57-85.

4. Authors Garretón and Cavarozzi developed the concept of sociopolitical matrix. Garretón, from a sociological perspective, initially used the metaphor of a "columna vertebral" and adopted the terms "matriz constituyente de actores sociales" and "matriz de constitución de la sociedad" in 1984, in *Dictaduras y Democratización* (Santiago de Chile: FLACSO); the term "sociopolitical matrix" (among others) in 1987, in *Reconstruir la Política* (Santiago de Chile: Editorial Andante); and, in 1991, in "Política, Cultura y Sociedad en la Transición Democrática," *Nueva Sociedad* (Caracas), no. 114 (July-August). See also, Garretón and Malva Espinosa, 1992, *¿Reforma del Estado o Cambios en la Matriz Sociopolítica?* (Santiago de Chile: FLACSO, Programa Chile). Marcelo Cavarozzi, writing within the political economy perspective, has used the term "state-centric matrix" to describe the predominant relations between the state and economy in an "inward-looking" development model. See his 1992 article, "Beyond Transitions to Democracy in Latin America," *Journal of Latin American Studies* 24 (3): 65-84.

Thus, the concept of the statist-national-popular matrix combines features of a "classic matrix" and of a "state-centric matrix." The classic matrix is more embedded in the sociology of action and in political science, while the state-centric matrix is based more in notions of political economy. The origin of the term "national-popular" can be attributed to Gino Germani, although he did not conceptualize it in exactly the same way as we do in this text; e.g., see Gino Germani, 1978, *Authoritarianism, Fascism, and National Populism* (New Brunswick, N.J.: Transaction Books). Touraine, 1989, also employs this concept.

5. Touraine, 1989.

6. For examples from Mexico, see Peter S. Cleaves, 1987, *The Professions and the State: The Mexican Case* (Tucson, Ariz.: University of Arizona Press).

7. Rosemary Thorp, 1992, "A Reappraisal of the Origins of Import-Substituting Industrialization, 1930-1950," *Journal of Latin American Studies* 24, quincentenary supplement: 181-196.

8. Published in English as United Nations, Economic Commission for Latin America, 1950, *The Economic Development of Latin America and Its Principal Problems* (Lake Success, N.Y.: United Nations Department of Economic Affairs). For an analysis of Prebisch's influence, see Alberto O. Hirschman, 1971, *A Bias for Hope: Essays on Development and Latin America* (New Haven, Conn.: Yale University Press), 270-297; Max Flores Diaz et al., 1981, *La Industrialización y Desarrollo en América Latina* (Caracas: Universidad Central de Venezuela, Facultad de Ciencias Económicas y Sociales, Instituto de Investigaciones Económicas y Sociales); Joseph L. Love, 1994, "Economic Ideas and Ideologies in Latin America since 1930," in *Cambridge History of Latin America* Vol. VI: Part I, ed. Leslie Bethell (Cambridge, U.K.: Cambridge University Press), 393-460; and the various articles in *Revista de la Cepal*, 2001, "Homenaje a Raúl Prebisch," No. 75 (Dec.): 7-113.

9. Also known by its Spanish acronym, CEPAL (Comisión Económica para América Latina).

10. For a discussion of business political motivations in the statist-national-popular SMP, see Peter S. Cleaves, 1995, "Empresarios y política empresarial en América Latina," in Alcántara and Crespo, 287-306.

11. See, for example, German W. Rama, ed., 1980, *Educación y Sociedad en América Latina y el Caribe* (Santiago de Chile: UNICEF); Rama, 1984, *El Sistema Educativo en América Latina* (Buenos Aires: Kapelusz); and Rama, ed., 1987, *Desarrollo y Educación en América Latina y el Caribe* (Buenos Aires: Kapelusz); David E. Lorey, 1992, *The Rise of the Professions in Twentieth-Century Mexico: University Graduates and Occupational Change since 1929* (Los Angeles: UCLA Latin American Center Publications).

12. See Jorge Graciarena, 1967, *Poder y Clases Sociales en el Desarrollo de América Latina* (Buenos Aires: Paidos); Francisco C. Weffort and Aníbal Quijano, 1976, *Populismo, Marginalización y Dependencia: Ensayos de Interpretación Sociológica* (San José, Costa Rica: Editorial Universitaria); Fernando Henrique Cardoso and Enzo Faletto, 1979, *Dependency and Development in Latin America* (Berkeley, Calif.: University of California Press); Tomás Moulián, 1984, *Tensiones y Crisis Política: Análisis de la Década del Sesenta* (Santiago, Chile: Centro de Estudios del Desarrollo); Alain Touraine, 1987, *Actores Sociales y Sistemas Políticos en América Latina* (Santiago de Chile: PREALC); Manuel A. Garretón, 1988, *The Chilean Political Process* (Boston: Unwin Hyman); and Paul Cammack, 1994, "Democratization and Citizenship in Latin America," in Geraint Parry and Michael Moran, eds., *Democracy and Democratization* (London: Routledge), 174-195.

13. On this point, see Marcelo Cavarozzi's analysis (1986) of democratic exclusion in both military and civilian governments in "Peronism and Radicalism: Argentina's Transition in Perspective," in *Elections and Democratization in Latin America, 1980-1985*, eds. Paul W. Drake and Eduardo Silva (La Jolla, Calif.: Center for Iberian and Latin American Studies, University of California), 143-174.

14. For case studies, see Peter S. Cleaves, 1974, *Bureaucratic Politics and Administration in Chile* (Berkeley, Calif.: University of California Press).

15. The notion of a "permanent option" is drawn from Jonathan Hartlyn and Arturo Valenzuela, 1994, "Democracy in Latin America since 1930," in Bethell, 1994, 162.

16. On "statist politicization," see Cavarozzi, 1994.

17. See Sonia E. Alvarez, Evelina Dagnino, and Arturo Escobar, eds., 1998, *Cultures of Politics/Politics of Cultures: Revisioning Latin American Social Movements* (Boulder, Colo.: Westview Press).

18 . For example, see Marta Harnecker, 1978, *Los conceptos elementales del materialismo histórico* (México: Siglo Veintiuno Editores).

19. On globalization as a sociopolitical, cultural, and economic phenomenon, see Mike Featherstone, 1996, *Undoing Culture: The Globalization of Capitalism in Third World Countries* (Westport, Conn.: Praeger Publishers); Malcolm Waters, 1995, *Globalization* (London: Routledge); Arjun Appadurai, 1996, *Modernity at Large: Cultural Dimensions of Globalization* (Minneapolis: University of Minnesota Press); Paul Q. Hirst, 1996, *Globalization in Question: The International Political Economy and the Possibilities of Governance* (Cambridge, UK: Polity Press); Satya R. Pattnayak, ed., 1996, *Globalization, Urbanization, and the State: Selected Studies in Contemporary Latin America* (Lanham, Md.: University Press of America); Saskia Sassen, 1996, *Losing Control? Sovereignty in an Age of Globalization* (New York: Columbia University Press); Tony Spybey, 1996, *Globalization and World Society* (Cambridge, UK: Polity Press); Bryan R. Roberts, 1995, *The Making of Citizens: Cities of Peasants Revisited,* 2nd ed. (New York: Halsted Press); John Eade, 1997, *Living the Global City: Globalization as a Local Process* (New York: Routledge); Michael Hardt and Antonio Negri, 2000, *Empire* (Cambridge, Mass.: Harvard University Press); Jeffrey Stark, 1998, "Globalization and Democracy in Latin America," in *Fault Lines of Democracy in Post-Transition Latin America,* eds. Felipe Agüero and Jeffrey Stark (Coral Gables, Fla.: North-South Center Press at the University of Miami); Jacques Chonchol, 2000, *Hacia dónde nos lleva la globalización?* (Santiago: LOM Ediciones); Víctor Flores Olea and Abelardo Mariña Flores, 1999, *Crítica de la globalidad: Dominación y liberación en nuestro tiempo* (México D.F.: Fondo de Cultura Económica); and Joseph E. Stiglitz, 2002, *Globalization and Its Discontents* (New York: W.W. Norton).

20. See Gary Gereffi and Lynn Hempel, 1996, "Latin America in the Global Economy: Running Faster to Stay in Place," *NACLA — Report on the Americas* 29 (4): 18. For an elaboration of some of the ideas developed here, see Gary Gereffi, 1995, "Global Production Systems and Third World Development," in *Global Change, Regional Response: The New International Context of Development,* ed. Barbara Stallings (Cambridge, UK: Cambridge University Press).

21. Peter Dicken, 1998, *Global Shift: Transforming the World Economy,* 3rd ed. (New York: Guilford Publications).

22. See Nigel Harris, 1987, *The End of the Third World* (New York: Penguin Books).

23. The notion of global commodity chains focuses on the local context of global production and shows how globalization actually reinforces localization processes in the world economy. See Gary Gereffi and Miguel Korzeniewicz, 1994, *Commodity Chains and Global Capitalism* (Westport, Conn.: Praeger Publishers); and Gary Gereffi, 2001, "Shifting Governance Structures in Global Commodity Chains, with Special Reference to the Internet," *American Behavioral Scientist* 44 (10): 1616-1637.

24. See Gary Gereffi and Donald Wyman, eds., 1990, *Manufacturing Miracles: Paths of Industrialization in Latin America and East Asia* (Princeton, N.J.: Princeton University Press); and Gary Gereffi, 2003, "Mexico's Industrial

Development: Climbing Ahead or Falling Behind in the World Economy?" in *Confronting Development: Assessing Mexico's Economic and Social Policy Changes*, eds. Kevin Middlebrook and Eduardo Zepeda (Stanford, Calif.: Stanford University Press).

25. World Bank, 2002, "2001 World Development Indicators" (Washington, D.C.) at <http://www.worldbank.org/data/wdi2001/pdfs/tab4_2.pdf>.

26. Using the World Bank's criteria, "high-income, advanced industrial economies" are defined as all members of the Organization for Economic Cooperation and Development (OECD) with 1990 per capita incomes of US$7,620 or more. These criteria cover 19 nations. See World Bank, 1992, *World Development Report 1992* (New York: Oxford University Press).

27. International Monetary Fund, September 2002, *World Economic Outlook*, 167.

28. Trade data from the OECD, cited in Gereffi and Hempel, 1996.

29. Jorge M. Katz, ed., 1987, *Technology Generation in Latin American Manufacturing Industries* (New York: St. Martin's Press). See also World Bank, 2001, *World Development Report 2000/2001: Attacking Poverty* (Oxford: Oxford University Press), 184-185; whereas in 1987, fewer than 20 percent of biotechnology patents were held by the six largest corporations involved in this field, by 1999, these corporations held well over 60 percent of such patents, and it is estimated that 97 percent of all patents worldwide are registered in industrialized countries.

30. On global banking and finance, see Yusuke Kashiwagi, 1986, *The Emergence of Global Finance* (Washington, D.C.: Per Jacobson Foundation); Hazel J. Johnson, 1993, *Financial Institutions and Markets: A Global Perspective* (New York: McGraw-Hill); Ethan B. Kapstein, 1994, *Governing the Global Economy: International Finance and the State* (Cambridge, Mass.: Harvard University Press); Wolfgang H. Reinicke, 1995, *Banking, Politics, and Global Finance: American Commercial Banks and Regulatory Change, 1980-1990* (Aldershot, UK: Edward Elgar); Geoffrey R.D. Underhill, ed., 1996, *The New World Order in International Finance* (London: Macmillan Publishers).

31. On finance and investment in the postwar period, see Stephany Griffith-Jones, 1984, *International Finance and Latin America* (London: Croom Helm); Eric Helleiner, 1994, *States and the Reemergence of Global Finance: From Bretton Woods to the 1990s* (Ithaca, N.Y.: Cornell University Press); Ricardo Ffrench-Davis and Stephany Griffith-Jones, eds., 1995, *Coping with Capital Surges: The Return of Finance to Latin America* (Boulder, Colo.: Lynne Rienner Publishers).

32. On the debt crisis in Latin America, see Miguel S. Wionczek, 1985, *Politics and Economics of External Debt Crisis: The Latin American Experience* (Boulder, Colo.: Westview Press); Rosemary Thorp and Laurence Whitehead, eds., 1987, *Latin American Debt and the Adjustment Crisis* (Pittsburgh: University of Pittsburgh Press); Ernest J. Oliveri, 1992, *Latin American Debt and the Politics of International Finance* (Westport, Conn.: Praeger Publishers); and Robert Devlin,

1989, *Debt and Crisis in Latin America: The Supply Side of the Story* (Princeton, N.J.: Princeton University Press).

33. For one useful discussion, see Stephany Griffith-Jones and Barbara Stallings, 1995, "New Global Financial Trends: Implications for Development," in Stallings 1995, 143-173.

34. See Sebastian Edwards, 1995, *Crisis and Reform in Latin America: From Despair to Hope* (Oxford: Oxford University Press); Juan Antonio Morales and Gary McMahon, eds., 1996, *Economic Policy and the Transition to Democracy: The Latin American Experience* (New York: St. Martin's Press); Melissa H. Birch and Jerry Haar, eds., 1999, *The Impact of Privatization in Latin America* (Coral Gables, Fla.: North-South Center Press at the University of Miami); and Oxhorn et al., 1998.

35. Among other works, see Jesús Martín Barbero, 1993, translated by Elizabeth Fox and Robert A. White, *Communication, Culture and Hegemony: From the Media to Mediations* (London: Sage Publications, Inc.); Jesús Martín Barbero, Fabio López de la Roche, Jaime Eduardo Jaramillo, and Renato Ortiz, eds., 1999, *Cultura y globalización* (Bogotá: Universidad Nacional de Colombia, Centro de Estudios Sociales); Manuel Antonio Garretón, ed., 1999, *América Latina: un espacio cultural en el mundo globalizado, debates y perspectives* (Santafé de Bogotá: Convenio Andrés Bello); and Néstor García Canclini, 1999, *La globalización imaginada* (México, D.F.: Fondo de Cultura Económica).

36. Like the act itself, the definition of terrorism is subject to political interpretation. Under U.S. law, 22 U.S. Code Section 2656f(d), 2002, at <http://www4.law.cornell.edu/uscode/22/2656f.html>, for example, the term "terrorism" means premeditated, politically motivated violence perpetrated against noncombatant targets by subnational groups or clandestine agents, usually intended to influence an audience; the term "international terrorism" means terrorism involving citizens or the territory of more than one country; and the term "terrorist group" means any group practicing, or that has significant subgroups that practice, international terrorism. This definition, in turn, does not provide for "state terrorism," which has been practiced in Latin America when governments have kidnapped, murdered, or "eliminated" citizens without due process.

37. For a history of Carlos the Jackal, see John Follain, 1998, *Jackal: The Secret Wars of Carlos the Jackal* (London: Weidenfeld & Nicolson).

38. World Bank, 2001, 180.

39. David B. Yoffie, 1983, *Power and Protectionism: Strategies of the Newly Industrializing Countries* (New York: Columbia University Press).

40. The textile and apparel industries in Hong Kong offer an excellent illustration of this process. See Siu-Lun Wong, 1988, *Emigrant Entrepreneurs: Shanghai Industrialists in Hong Kong* (Hong Kong: Oxford University Press); and James Lardner, 1988, "The Sweater Trade — I," *The New Yorker*, January 11, 39-73.

41. See Gereffi, 2003, and Enrique Dussel Peters, 2000, *Polarizing Mexico: The Impact of Liberalization Strategy* (Boulder, Colo.: Lynne Rienner Publishers).

42. For a sample of the extensive literature on hemispheric trade, see Sidney Weintraub, ed., 1994, *Integrating the Americas: Shaping Future Trade Policy* (Coral Gables, Fla.: North-South Center Press at the University of Miami); Lincoln Bizzozer and Marcel Vaillant, eds., 1996, *La Inserción Internacional del MERCOSUR: Mirando al Sur o Mirando al Norte?* (Montevideo: Arca); João Paulo dos Reis Velloso, ed., 1995, *MERCOSUL e NAFTA: o Brasil e a Integração Hemisférica* (Rio de Janeiro: Olympio Editora); Roberto Bouzas and Jaime Ros, eds., 1994, *Economic Integration in the Western Hemisphere* (Notre Dame: University of Notre Dame Press); Ruud Buitelaar and Pitou van Dijck, 1996, *Latin America's Insertion in the World Economy: Towards Systemic Competitiveness in Small Economies* (New York: St. Martin's Press); Frederick W. Mayer, 1998, *Interpreting NAFTA: The Science and Art of Political Analysis* (New York: Columbia University); Riordan Roett, 1999, *Mercosur: Regional Integration, World Markets* (Boulder, Colo.: Lynne Rienner Publishers); Gordon Mace and Louis Bélanger, eds., 1999, *The Americas in Transition: The Contours of Regionalism* (Boulder, Colo.: Lynne Rienner Publishers); and Gary Gereffi, David Spener, and Jennifer Bair, eds., 2002, *Free Trade and Uneven Development: The North American Apparel Industry After NAFTA* (Philadelphia: Temple University Press).

43. See Francisco Durand and Eduardo Silva, eds., 1998, *Organized Business, Economic Change, and Democracy in Latin America* (Coral Gables, Fla.: North-South Center Press at the University of Miami). Also, Eduardo Silva, 1998, *The State and Capital in Chile: Business Elites, Technocrats, and Market Economics* (Boulder, Colo.: Westview Press).

44. See Albert Fishlow, 1985, "Lessons from the Past: Capital Markets during the 19th Century and the Interwar Period," *International Organization* 39 (3): 394.

45. Fishlow, 1985, 419.

46. For an insightful analysis of the origins of political regimes — liberal democracy, social democracy, fascism, and traditional dictatorship — in interwar Europe, see Gregory Luebbert, 1991, *Liberalism, Fascism, or Social Democracy: Social Classes and Political Origins of Regimes in Interwar Europe* (Oxford: Oxford University Press).

47. See Carlos Díaz-Alejandro, 1980, *Latin America in Depression*, Discussion Paper no. 344: March (New Haven, Conn.: Yale University Economic Growth Center); and Carlos Díaz-Alejandro, 1981, *Some Lessons of the 1930s for the 1980s*, Discussion Paper no. 376: April (New Haven, Conn.: Yale University Economic Growth Center).

48. Díaz-Alejandro, 1981.

49. See Gøsta Esping-Andersen, 1990, *The Three Worlds of Welfare Capitalism* (Princeton, N.J.: Princeton University Press) for an analysis of the emergence of three different models of welfare regimes in the advanced capitalist countries in the post-war period; for a recent analysis, see Evelyne Huber and John D. Stephens,

2001, *Development and Crisis of the Welfare State: Parties and Policies in Global Markets* (Chicago: University of Chicago Press).

50. See Helen Milner, 1997, *Interests, Institutions, and Information* (Princeton, N.J.: Princeton University Press) for a detailed explanation of the bargaining processes leading to the creation of the International Monetary Fund and the failure in reaching an agreement around the International Trade Organization.

51. See José María Fanelli, Roberto Frenkel, and Guillermo Rozenwurcel, 1990, *Growth and Structural Reform in Latin America: Where Do We Stand?* (Buenos Aires: CEDES).

52. See Marcelo Cavarozzi, 1982, "El 'desarrollismo' y las relaciones entre democracia y capitalismo dependiente en 'Dependencia y desarrollo en América Latina,'" *Latin American Research Review* 17 (3): 166-171.

53. On market economies, the "Washington Consensus," and the neoliberal economic model, see CORDES, 1987, *Neoliberalismo y Políticas Económicas Alternativas* (Quito: Corporación de Estudios para el Desarrollo); John Williamson, ed., 1990, *Latin American Adjustment: How Much Has Happened?* (Washington, D.C.: Institute for International Economics); Rudiger Dornbusch, 1991, "Structural Adjustment in Latin America," Latin American Program Working Paper no. 191 (Washington, D.C.: The Wilson Center); John Williamson, 1993, "Democracy and the 'Washington Consensus,'" *World Development* 21 (8): 1329-1337; Walden F. Bello, 1994, *Dark Victory: The United States, Structural Adjustment, and Global Poverty* (London: Pluto Press); William C. Smith et al., 1994a and 1994b; Daniel M. Schydlowsky, 1995, *Structural Adjustment: Retrospect and Prospect* (Westport, Conn.: Praeger Publishers); and Albert Berry, ed., 1998, *Poverty, Economic Reform, and Income Distribution in Latin America* (Boulder, Colo.: Lynne Rienner Publishers).

54. Alain Touraine, 1964, *Social Mobility, Class Relationship and Nationalism in Latin America*, Documento de Trabajo no. 13 (Buenos Aires: Instituto Torcuato di Tella, Centro de Sociología Comparada).

55. Henry Veltmeyer and James Petras, 1997, emphasize this point in *Neoliberalism and Class Conflict in Latin America: A Comparative Perspective on the Political Economy of Structural Adjustment* (New York: St. Martin's Press). See also, James L. Dietz, ed., 1995, *Latin America's Economic Development: Confronting Crisis* (Boulder, Colo.: Lynne Rienner Publishers); and Atilio Borón, 1995, *State, Capitalism, and Democracy in Latin America* (Boulder, Colo.: Lynne Rienner Publishers).

56. For example, see the essays in William C. Smith and Roberto Patricio Korzeniewicz, eds., 1997, *Politics, Social Change, and Economic Restructuring in Latin America* (Coral Gables, Fla.: North-South Center Press at the University of Miami).

57. The literature on democracy and democratization is extensive. See, for example, Dankwart A. Rustow, 1970, "Transitions to Democracy: Toward a Dynamic Model," *Comparative Politics* 2 (April): 337-363; Robert A. Dahl, 1971,

Polyarchy: Participation and Opposition (New Haven, Conn.: Yale University Press); Samuel P. Huntington, 1984, "Will More Countries Become Democratic?" *Political Science Quarterly* 99 (Summer): 193-218; Guillermo O'Donnell, Philippe C. Schmitter, and Laurence Whitehead, 1986, *Transitions from Authoritarian Rule*, four volumes (Baltimore: The Johns Hopkins University Press); Larry Diamond, Jonathan Hartlyn, Juan J. Linz, and Seymour Martin Lipset, eds., 1999, *Democracy in Developing Countries: Latin America*, 2nd ed. (Boulder, Colo.: Lynne Rienner Publishers); and Terry Lynn Karl, 1990, "Dilemmas of Democratization in Latin America," *Comparative Politics* 23 (1): 1-21.

58. See Marcelo Cavarozzi, 1994, "Politics: A Key for the Long Term in South America," in Smith et al. 1994b.

59. See Jonathan Hartlyn, 1997, "Democracy in South America: Convergences and Diversities," in *Argentina: The Challenges of Modernization*, eds. Joseph S. Tulchin and Allison Garland (Wilmington, Del.: Scholarly Resources, Inc.).

60. Samuel P. Huntington, 1991, *The Third Wave: Democratization in the Late Twentieth Century* (Norman, Okla.: University of Oklahoma Press). See also Philippe C. Schmitter, 1991, "Cinco reflexiones sobre la cuarta onda de democratizaciones," in *Transiciones a la Democracia en Europa y América Latina*, eds. Carlos Barba Solano, José Luis Barros, and Javier Hurtado (Mexico City: M.A. Porrua Grupo Editorial).

61. Manuel A. Garretón, 1995b, *Hacia una Nueva Era Política: Estudio sobre las Democratizaciones* (Mexico City: Fondo de Cultura Económica).

62. On democratic transitions, see O'Donnell et al., 1986; Manuel A. Garretón, 1989, "Las Transiciones a la Democracia y el Caso Chileno," Discussion Paper no. 116 (Santiago de Chile: FLACSO); Metin Heper, 1991, "Transitions to Democracy Reconsidered," in *Comparative Political Dynamics*, eds. Dankwart A. Rustow and Kenneth Paul Erickson (New York: HarperCollins), 192-210; Nancy Bermeo, 1992, "Democracy and the Lessons of Dictatorship," *Comparative Politics* 23 (3): 273-292; Gretchen Casper and Michelle M. Taylor, eds., 1996, *Negotiating Democracy: Transitions from Authoritarian Rule* (Pittsburgh: University of Pittsburgh Press); and Juan J. Linz and Alfred Stepan, 1996, *Problems of Democratic Transition and Consolidation: Southern Europe, South America, and Post-Communist Europe* (Baltimore: The Johns Hopkins University Press).

63. On democratic consolidation, see J. Samuel Valenzuela, 1990, "Democratic Consolidation in Post-Transitional Settings: Notion, Process, and Facilitating Conditions," Working Paper no. 150 (Notre Dame, Ind.: Helen Kellogg Institute for International Studies, University of Notre Dame); John Higley and Richard Gunther, eds., 1992, *Elites and Democratic Consolidation in Latin America and Southern Europe* (New York: Cambridge University Press); Scott Mainwaring, Guillermo O'Donnell, and J. Samuel Valenzuela, eds., 1992, *Issues in Democratic Consolidation: The New South American Democracies in Comparative Perspective* (Notre Dame, Ind.: University of Notre Dame Press); Garretón, 1995b; Juan J. Linz, 1996, "Toward Consolidated Democracies," *Journal of Democracy* 7 (2): 14-34; Linz et al., 1996; Andreas Schedler, 1998, "What Is Democratic Consolidation?" *Journal*

of Democracy 9 (2): 91-107; and Jonathan Hartlyn, 2002, "Democracy and Consolidation in Contemporary Latin America: Current Thinking and Future Challenges," in Joseph Tulchin, ed., *Democratic Governance and Social Inequality* (Boulder, Colo.: Lynne Rienner Publishers), 103-130.

64. See various chapters in David Pion-Berlin, ed., 2001, *Civil-Military Relations in Latin America: New Analytical Perspectives* (Chapel Hill, N.C.: University of North Carolina Press).

65. O'Donnell et al., 1986.

66. The institutional context within which this "fencing" takes place can be created by the regime itself, as in the Brazilian and Chilean cases, or by precedent and on the part of civilians, as in Argentina and Peru. In Brazil, the military periodically changed the rules of the game through its so-called Institutional Acts. In Chile, the Pinochet dictatorship created its own Constitution, which made negotiating the transition extremely complex and gave the military considerable room to maneuver. In Argentina, the institutional mechanism for transition already was formalized in the existing Constitution, and discussion revolved around dates and procedures. In Peru, during the last stage of the military regime, the rules were written essentially by civilians in the form of a new Constitution.

67. These can be institutional (constitution, laws); symbolic and ethical (truth and justice relating to human rights violations under the military regime); actor based (civilian or military holdouts against democratic procedures); and cultural (values, styles, behaviors). See Garretón 1995b.

68. See Tommie Sue Montgomery, ed., 2000, *Peacemaking and Democratization in the Western Hemisphere* (Coral Gables, Fla.: North-South Center Press at the University of Miami).

69. See Bruce M. Bagley and William O. Walker III, eds., 1994, *Drug Trafficking in the Americas* (Coral Gables, Fla.: North-South Center Press at the University of Miami); Elizabeth Joyce and Carlos Malamud, eds., 1997, *Latin America and the Multinational Drug Trade* (New York: St. Martin's Press); Daniel Levy and Kathleen Bruhn, 1999, "Mexico: Sustained Civilian Rule and the Question of Democracy," in *Democracy in Developing Countries: Latin America*, 2nd ed., eds. Larry Diamond, Jonathan Hartlyn, Juan J. Linz, and Seymour Martin Lipset (Boulder, Colo.: Lynne Rienner Publishers); and Jonathan Hartlyn and John Dugas, 1999, "Colombia: The Politics of Violence and Democratic Transformation," in *Democracy in Developing Countries: Latin America*, eds. Larry Diamond et al.

70. Juan J. Linz, 1973, "The Future of an Authoritarian Situation or the Institutionalization of an Authoritarian Regime: The Case of Brazil," in *Authoritarian Brazil: Origins, Policies, and Future*, ed. Alfred Stepan (New Haven, Conn.: Yale University Press), 233-254.

71. Throughout this text, the Cuban case is mainly left aside because it corresponds to a different SPM from the one predominant in the rest of the region. Paradoxically, none of the phenomena analyzed for the statist-national-popular

matrix can be understood without taking into account the influence of the Cuban case, in terms of the reactions and counter-reactions it helped spark throughout the continent.

72. Abraham F. Lowenthal, ed., 1991, *Exporting Democracy: The United States and Latin America* (Baltimore: The Johns Hopkins University Press). The ambiguous actions of the George W. Bush administration in the hours following the short-lived coup attempt in Venezuela against President Hugo Chávez, in April 2002, highlight the continuing fragility of even this limited consensus.

73. See Margaret Keck and Kathryn Sikkink, 1998, *Activists Beyond Borders: Advocacy Networks in International Politics* (Ithaca, N.Y.: Cornell University Press); and Thomas Risse, Stephen C. Ropp, and Kathryn Sikkink, eds., 1999, *The Power of Human Rights: International Norms and Domestic Change* (Cambridge, UK: Cambridge University Press).

74. Marcelo Cavarozzi, 1995, "Los partidos políticos latinoamericanos, sus configuraciones históricas y su papel en las transiciones recientes," in *Los Límites de la Consolidación Democrática en América Latina*, eds. Manuel Alcántara and Ismael Crespo (Salamanca, Spain: Ediciones Universidad de Salamanca), 145-157.

75. The literature on the military in Latin America is extensive. See, for example, David Pion-Berlin, ed., 2001, as well as Samuel P. Huntington, 1968, *Political Order in Changing Societies* (New Haven: Yale University Press); Alfred Stepan, 1970, *The Military in Politics: Changing Patterns in Brazil* (Princeton, N.J.: Princeton University Press); Frederick M. Nunn, 1976, *The Military in Chilean History: Essays on Civil-Military Relations, 1810-1973* (Albuquerque, N.M.: University of New Mexico Press); Abraham F. Lowenthal and J. Samuel Fitch, eds., 1986, *Armies and Politics in Latin America* (New York: Holmes and Meier); Alfred Stepan, 1988, *Rethinking Military Politics: Brazil and the Southern Cone* (Princeton, N.J.: Princeton University Press); Frederick M. Nunn, 1992, *The Time of the Generals: Latin American Professional Militarism in World Perspective* (Lincoln, Neb.: University of Nebraska Press); Linda Alexander Rodriguez, ed., 1994, *Rank and Privilege: The Military and Society in Latin America* (Wilmington, Del.: Scholarly Resources); Richard L. Millett and Michael Gold-Biss, eds., 1996, *Beyond Praetorianism: The Latin American Military in Transition* (Coral Gables, Fla.: North-South Center Press at the University of Miami); Russell W. Ramsey, 1997, *Guardians of the Other Americas: Essays on the Military Forces of Latin America* (Lanham, Md.: University Press of America); and Brian Loveman and Thomas M. Davies, Jr., eds., 1996, *The Politics of Antipolitics: The Military in Latin America*, 3rd ed. (Washington, D.C.: Scholarly Resources).

76. This theme underlies the volume by Lars Schoultz, William C. Smith, and Augusto Varas, eds., 1994, *Security, Democracy, and Development in U.S.-Latin American Relations* (Coral Gables, Fla.: North-South Center Press at the University of Miami).

77. See Wendy Hunter, 1996, *State and Soldier in Latin America: Redefining the Military's Role in Argentina, Brazil, and Chile*, Peaceworks No. 10 (Washington, D.C.: United States Institute of Peace), especially Chapter 5.

78. For a typology of civil-military relations and analyses of the variations across countries and of patterns of movement within countries, see J. Samuel Fitch, 1991, "Democracy, Human Rights, and the Armed Forces in Latin America," in *The United States and Latin America in the 1990s: Beyond the Cold War*, eds. Jonathan Hartlyn, Lars Schoultz, and Augusto Varas (Chapel Hill, N.C.: University of North Carolina Press), 192-195.

79. For recent analyses examining constraints on military behavior, see Wendy Hunter, 1997, *Eroding Military Influence in Brazil: Politicians Against Soldiers* (Chapel Hill, N.C.: University of North Carolina Press); and David Pion-Berlin, 1997, *Through Corridors of Power: Institutions and Civil-Military Relations in Argentina* (University Park, Pa.: Pennsylvania State University Press).

80. On this point, see Guillermo O'Donnell, 1994a, "Delegative Democracy," *Journal of Democracy* 5 (1): 55-69; Francisco C. Weffort, 1992, *New Democracies, Which Democracies?* (Washington, D.C.: The Wilson Center Latin American Program, The Woodrow Wilson International Center for Scholars); and Larry Diamond, 1999, *Developing Democracy: Toward Consolidation* (Baltimore: The Johns Hopkins University Press). See also Barba Solano et al., 1991; José Luis Barros, Javier Hurtado, and German Pérez Fernández del Castillo, eds., 1991, *Transición a la Democracia y Reforma del Estado en México* (Mexico City: M.A. Porrua Grupo Editorial); and David Collier and Steven Levitsky, 1997, "Democracy with 'Adjectives,'" *World Politics* 49 (3): 430-452; Agüero and Stark, 1998.

81. Valuable works examining recent trends regarding social inequality and societal responses include Douglas Chalmers, et al., eds., 1997, *The New Politics of Inequality in Latin America: Rethinking Participation and Representation* (Oxford: Oxford University Press); Nora Lustig, ed., 1995, *Coping with Austerity: Poverty and Inequality in Latin America* (Washington, D.C.: The Brookings Institution); CEPAL, 1992, *Equidad y Transformación Productiva: Un Enfoque Integrado* (Santiago: CEPAL); and UN ECLAC, 2000, *Equity, Development and Citizenship*, presented to the 28th session, Mexico City, April 3-7 (Santiago: ECLAC).

82. One notable study is Alejandro Portes, 1995, *En Torno a la Informalidad: Ensayo sobre Teoría y Medición de la Economía No Regulada* (Mexico City: M.A. Porrúa Grupo Editorial). See also George Psacharopoulos et al., 1997, *Poverty and Income Distribution in Latin America: The Story of the 1980s* (Washington, D.C.: The World Bank); Inter-American Development Bank, 1998, *Facing Up to Inequality in Latin America: Economic and Social Progress in Latin America 1998-1999 Report* (Washington, D.C.: IDB, distributed by The Johns Hopkins University Press); Victor E. Tokman and Guillermo O'Donnell, eds., 1998, *Poverty and Inequality in Latin America: Issues and New Challenges* (Notre Dame, Ind.: University of Notre Dame Press); Carlos H. Filgueira, 2001, *La actualidad de viejas temáticas: sobre los estudios de clase, estratificación y movilidad en América Latina*, Serie Políticas Sociales, no. 51 (Santiago de Chile: CEPAL); and the recent annual issues of CEPAL, *Panorama Social de América Latina* (Santiago de Chile: CEPAL).

83. IDB, 1998, 14-15.

84. CEPAL, 2001, *Panorama Social de América Latina, 2000-2001* (Santiago), 67-84.

85. Inter-American Development Bank (IDB), 2000, *Development Beyond Economics: Economic and Social Progress in Latin America 2000 Report* (Washington, D.C.: IDB, distributed by The Johns Hopkins University Press), 71-72.

86. A fundamental divergence between Latin America and Asia has been vastly greater investments in education and human capital carried out by East Asian states. For example, high school enrollment rates in East Asia grew from 34 percent in 1965 to 86 percent in 1992, while in Latin America, they only grew from 19 percent to 47 percent over this same period. See Barbara Stallings, 1995, "Introduction," 30.

87. For the modernity-identity debate, see Nestor Garcia Canclini, 1995, *Hybrid Cultures: Strategies for Entering and Leaving Modernity*, translated by Christopher L. Chiappari and Silvia L. Lopez (Minneapolis: University of Minnesota Press); Rigoberto Lanz, ed., 1993, *La Discusión Posmoderna* (Caracas: Fondo Editorial Tropykos); Frans J. Schuurman, ed., 1993, *Beyond the Impasse: New Directions in Development Theory* (London: Zed Books); Jorge Larraín, 1996, *Modernidad, Razón e Identidad en América Latina* (Santiago: Editorial Andres Bello); and Martín Hopenhayn, 2001, *No Apocalypse, No Integration: Modernism and Postmodernism in Latin America*, translated by Cynthia Margarita Tompkins and Elizabeth Rosa Horan (Durham, N.C.: Duke University Press).

88. See Daniel H. Levine, ed., 1993, *Constructing Culture and Power in Latin America* (Ann Arbor, Mich.: University of Michigan Press).

89. Fernando Fajnzylber began to develop these concepts prior to his untimely death. See his 1990 book, *Unavoidable Industrial Restructuring in Latin America* (Durham, N.C.: Duke University Press).

90. For an initial statement of the "Washington Consensus" policy measures, see Williamson, 1990, chapter 2; for a synthetic review of reforms in Chile, see Javier Martínez and Alvaro Díaz, 1996, *Chile: The Great Transformation* (Washington, D.C.: The Brookings Institution and the UN Research Institute for Social Development); and for such a review covering three major Latin American countries, see Judith A. Teichman, 2001, *The Politics of Freeing Markets in Latin America: Chile, Argentina, and Mexico* (Chapel Hill, N.C.: University of North Carolina Press). Also useful is William P. Glade and Rossana Corona, eds., 1996, *Bigger Economies, Smaller Governments: Privatization in Latin America* (Boulder, Colo.: Westview Press).

91. For example, see *The Economist,* 1997, "The World Economy Survey" 20 (September). *The Economist* is among the strongest proponents of economic liberalism. Though asserting in this survey a preference for political democracy to any other form of government, the editors did so reluctantly because they viewed democracy as a greater threat to economic liberty than they saw capitalism as a threat

to democracy. They further asserted that arguments that the power of the state has declined (which they would strongly favor) tend to be grossly exaggerated.

92. See Linz and Stepan, 1996, 11-13.

93. For a comprehensive comparison of these two regions, see Gereffi and Wyman, eds., 1990.

94. See UN ECLAC, 2001, *Preliminary Overview of the Economies of Latin America and the Caribbean 2001* (Santiago: ECLAC), 7.

95. For examples of grassroots culture linked to social processes, see Charles David Kleymeyer, ed., 1994, *Cultural Expression and Grassroots Development: Cases from Latin America and the Caribbean* (Boulder, Colo.: Lynne Rienner Publishers).

96. In addition to criticizing aspects of the previous economic model, which it once championed, CEPAL has proposed a new vision for achieving economic transformation with equity in Latin America. For examples, see CEPAL, 1992, and UN ECLAC, 2000. See also Ricardo Ffrench-Davis, 1999, *Macroeconomía, comercio y finanzas: Para reformar las reformas en América Latina* (Santiago: McGraw-Hill). More radical visions have been presented at the World Social Forum, which met in Porto Alegre, Brazil, in January 2001, January 2002, and January 2003. See the various documents posted at www.forumsocialmundial.org.br. On the evolving vision of the World Bank, see The World Bank, 2002, *World Development Report 2002: Building Institutions for Markets* (Washington, D.C.: The World Bank).

97. See Ffrench-Davis, 1999, and also Ricardo Ffrench-Davis, ed., 1999, *Entre el Neoliberalismo y el crecimiento con equidad* (Santiago: Dolmen Ediciones).

98. On presidentialism in Latin America, see Juan J. Linz et al., eds., 1990, *Hacia una Democracia Moderna: La Opción Parlamentaria* (Santiago: Ediciones Universidad Católica de Chile); Dieter Nohlen and Mario Fernández, eds., 1991, *Presidencialismo versus Parlamentarismo, América Latina* (Caracas: Editorial Nueva Sociedad); Juan J. Linz and Arturo Valenzuela, eds., 1994, *The Failure of Presidential Democracy* (Baltimore: The Johns Hopkins University Press); Scott Mainwaring and Matthew Shugart, eds., 1997b, *Presidentialism and Democracy in Latin America* (Cambridge, UK: Cambridge University Press); and Scott Mainwaring and Matthew Shugart, 1997a, "Juan Linz, Presidentialism, and Democracy: A Critical Appraisal," *Comparative Politics* (July): 449-471. For an argument that controlling for per capita income, parliamentary systems endure longer than presidential ones (the United States, of course, being a major exception), see Adam Przeworski et al., 2000, *Democracy and Development: Political Institutions and Well-being in the World, 1950-1990* (Cambridge, UK: Cambridge University Press), 128-132.

99. Parts of this paragraph and the next one draw on Jonathan Hartlyn, 2001, "Constitutional Powers: Legislative Power and Its Relation to Executive Power," prepared for presentation at the Conference on Democratic Transition and Consolidation, Madrid, October, 18-20.

100. This is similar to the idea expressed by Guillermo O'Donnell with respect to the necessity to extend and deepen the "rule of law" where it is absent or precarious in diverse spheres of society or in entire societies. See O'Donnell, 1994b, "Some Reflections on Redefining the Role of the State," in *Redefining the State in Latin America*, ed. Colin I. Bradford (Paris: Organization for Economic Cooperation and Development), 251-260; and Juan E. Méndez, Guillermo O'Donnell, and Paulo Sérgio Pinheiro, eds., 1999, *The Rule of Law and the Underprivileged in Latin America* (Notre Dame, Ind.: University of Notre Dame Press).

101. For Mexico, see Victoria E. Rodríguez, 1997, *Decentralization in Mexico: From Reforma Municipal to Solidaridad to Nuevo Federalismo* (Boulder, Colo.: Westview Press). For Brazil, see Celina Souza, 1997, *Constitutional Engineering in Brazil: The Politics of Federalism and Decentralization* (New York: St. Martin's Press). Also, Menno Vellinga, ed., 1997, *The Changing Role of the State in Latin America* (Boulder, Colo.: Westview Press); and Peter Spink and Luiz Carlos Bresser-Pereira, eds., 1998, *Reforma do Estado e Administração Pública Gerencial* (Rio de Janeiro: Fundação Getúlio Vargas).

102. Larry Diamond, Jonathan Hartlyn, and Juan J. Linz, 1999, "Introduction: Politics, Society, and Democracy in Latin America," in Diamond et al., 1999, 18-19; see also Peter M. Ward and Victoria E. Rodríguez, 1999, *New Federalism and State Government in Mexico: Bringing the States Back In* (Austin, Texas: Lyndon B. Johnson School of Public Affairs, University of Texas at Austin).

103. See Joseph S. Tulchin and Allison M. Garland, eds., 2000, *Social Development in Latin America: The Politics of Reform* (Boulder, Colo.: Lynne Rienner Publishers); and Mario Dos Santos, 1994, *Estrategias de gobernabilidad en la crisis*, Project Report RLA 90/011, UNDP-UNESCO-CLACSO (June).

104. See Evelyne Huber, 1995, *Options for Social Policy in Latin America: Neoliberal versus Social Democratic Models*, Discussion Paper 66, June (Geneva: United Nations Research Institute for Social Development). Other related works are the Inter-American Development Bank Forum on Social Reform and Poverty, 1993, *Social Reform and Poverty: Toward a Comprehensive Agenda for Development* (Washington, D.C.: Inter-American Development Bank); *World Development Report 1997: The State in a Changing World*, 1997 (Washington, D.C.: The World Bank); Bradford, 1994; and Bernardo Kliksberg, 1997, *Como Enfrentar los Déficits Sociales de América Latina* (San José, Costa Rica: FLACSO).

105. See Méndez et al., 1999, and Adolfo Aguilar Zinser, 2001, "Mexico's Security Challenges," *Update on the Americas*, No. 2: December (Washington, D.C.: Woodrow Wilson Center).

106. Kenneth M. Roberts and Erik Wibbels, 1999, "Party Systems and Electoral Volatility in Latin America: A Test of Economic, Institutional, and Structural Explanations," *American Political Science Review* 93 (3): 575-590.

107. Roberts et al., 1999, 575-590, see especially p. 585; see also Michael Coppedge, 1998, "The Evolution of Latin American Party Systems," in Scott Mainwaring and Arturo Valenzuela, eds., 1998, *Politics, Society, and Democracy: Latin America* (Boulder, Colo.: Westview Press), 171-206. Over the past several

years, the Colombian party system has been experiencing declining and atomized bipartyism, combined with a growing presence of highly fragmented third forces; this was especially evident in the presidential election of Alvaro Uribe in 2002, a Liberal who successfully challenged the machinery of his own party while receiving support from many Conservatives. See Ana María Bejarano and Eduardo Pizarro, 2001, "Reforma política después de 1991: ¿qué queda por reformar?" paper presented to a conference at the Helen Kellogg Institute for International Studies, University of Notre Dame, March.

108. See Scott P. Mainwaring, 1999, *Rethinking Party Systems in the Third Wave of Democratization: The Case of Brazil* (Stanford, Calif.: Stanford University Press); Marcelo Cavarozzi and Juan Abel Medina, eds., 2002, *El asedio a la política: Los partidos latinoamericanos en la era neoliberal* (Buenos Aires: Editorial Politeia); and J. Mark Payne, Daniel Zovatto G., Fernando Carrillo Flórez, Andrés Allamand Zavala, 2002, *Democracies in Development: Politics and Reform in Latin America* (Washington, D.C.: IDB and IDEA).

109. On movementism, see James McGuire, 1997, *Peronism without Perón: Unions, Parties, and Democracy in Argentina* (Stanford, Calif.: Stanford University Press). Exceptions include Uruguay and Chile.

110. See Rachel Meneguello, 2002, "Brasil," in *El asedio a la política: Los partidos latinoamericanos en la era neoliberal*, eds. Marcelo Cavarozzi and Juan Abel Medina (Buenos Aires: Editorial Politeia).

111. On political parties, see Cavarozzi, 1986; Arturo Valenzuela and J. Samuel Valenzuela, 1986, "Party Oppositions under the Chilean Authoritarian Regime," in *Military Rule in Chile: Dictatorship and Opposition*, eds. Samuel Valenzuela and Arturo Valenzuela (Baltimore: The Johns Hopkins University Press), 184-229; Cavarozzi and Garretón, eds., 1989, *Muerte y Resurrección: Los Partidos Políticos en el Autoritarismo y las Transiciones en el Cono Sur* (Santiago: FLACSO); Dieter Nohlen, ed., 1993, *Elecciones y Sistemas de Partidos en América Latina* (San José, Costa Rica: Instituto Interamericano de Derechos Humanos); Scott Mainwaring and Timothy Scully, eds., 1995, *Building Democratic Institutions: Party Systems in Latin America* (Stanford, Calif.: Stanford University Press); and Mainwaring, 1999.

112. On corruption, see James C. Scott, 1972, *Comparative Political Corruption*, (Englewood Cliffs, N.J.: Prentice-Hall); Robert E. Klitgaard, 1988, *Controlling Corruption* (Berkeley, Calif.: University of California Press); Robin Theobold, 1990, *Corruption, Development, and Underdevelopment* (London: Macmillan); Stephen D. Morris, 1991, *Corruption and Politics in Contemporary Mexico* (Tuscaloosa, Ala.: University of Alabama Press); Rafael Ballén, 1994, *Corrupción Política* (Bogotá: Ediciones Acropolis); Walter Little and Eduardo Posada-Carbó, eds., 1996, *Political Corruption in Latin America and Europe* (New York: St. Martin's Press); and Luigi Manzetti, 1994, "Latin America: Privatization, Property Rights, and Deregulation" *Quarterly Review of Economics and Finance Annual* 34: 43-77.

113. On the mass media, see Martin Carnoy et al., 1993, *The New Global Economy in the Information Age: Reflections on a Changing World* (University Park, Pa.: Pennsylvania State University Press); Emile G. McAnany and Kenton T. Wilkinson, eds., 1996, *Mass Media and Free Trade: NAFTA and the Cultural Industries* (Austin, Texas: University of Texas Press); and for media and democracy, see Elizabeth Fox, ed., 1988, *Media and Politics in Latin America: The Struggle for Democracy* (Newbury Park, Calif.: Sage Publications, Inc.); Marc Raboy and Bernard Dagenais, eds., 1992, *Media, Crisis, and Democracy: Mass Communication and the Disruption of Social Order* (Newbury Park, Calif.: Sage Publications, Inc.); and Carlos H. Filgueira and Dieter Nohlen, eds., 1994, *Prensa y Transición Democrática: Experiencias Recientes en Europa y América Latina* (Frankfurt: Vervuert).

114. For a classic discussion of governability, see Huntington, 1968; see also Manuel Alcántara Sáez, 1994, *Gobernabilidad, crisis y cambio: elementos para el estudio de la gobernabilidad de los sistemas políticos en épocas de crisis y cambio* (Madrid: Centro de Estudios Constitucionales).

115. See, among others, Marcelo Cavarozzi et al., 1989; and José E. Corradi, Patricia Weiss Fagen, and Manuel Antonio Garretón, eds., 1992, *Fear at the Edge: State Terror and Resistance in Latin America* (Berkeley, Calif.: University of California Press); Elizabeth Jelin and Eric Hershberg, eds., 1996, *Constructing Democracy: Human Rights, Citizenship, and Society in Latin America* (Boulder, Colo.: Westview Press); Susan Eckstein, ed., 2001, *Power and Popular Protest: Latin American Social Movements*, updated and expanded edition (Berkeley, Calif.: University of California Press).

116. On civil society, see Alfred Stepan, 1985, "State Power and the Strength of Civil Society in the Southern Cone of Latin America," in *Bringing the State Back In*, eds. Peter B. Evans, Dietrich Rueschemeyer, and Theda Skocpol (Cambridge, UK: Cambridge University Press), 317-347; Alfred Stepan, ed., 1989, *Democratizing Brazil: Problems of Transition and Consolidation* (New York: Oxford University Press); Víctor Pérez Díaz, 1993, *La Primacia de la Sociedad Civil: El Proceso de Formación de la España Democrática* (Madrid: Alianza Editorial); Leonardo Avritzer, ed., 1994, *Sociedade Civil e Democratização* (Belo Horizonte: Livraria del Rey Editora); Philip Oxhorn, 1995, *Organizing Civil Society: The Popular Sectors and the Struggle for Democracy in Chile* (University Park, Pa.: Pennsylvania State University Press); and Manuel Antonio Garretón M., 2002, "La transformación de la acción colectiva en América Latina," *Revista de la CEPAL* 76 (April): 7-24. On "new social movements," see Jean L. Cohen, 1983, "Rethinking Social Movements," *Berkeley Journal of Sociology* 28: 97-114; Scott P. Mainwaring and Eduardo Viola, 1984, "New Social Movements, Political Culture, and Democracy: Brazil and Argentina in the 1980s" *Telos* no. 61 (Fall): 17-54; Scott P. Mainwaring, 1987, "Urban Popular Movements, Identity, and Democratization in Brazil" *Comparative Political Studies* 20 (2): 131-159; Bronislaw Misztal and Barbara A. Misztal, 1988, "Democratization Processes as an Objective of New Social Movements," *Research in Social Movements, Conflicts and Change* 10: 93-106; Charles Tilly, 1988, "Social Movements, Old and New" *Research in Social Movements, Conflicts and Change* 10: 1-18; Marta Fuentes and André Gunder

Frank, 1989, "Ten Theses on Social Movements" *World Development* 17 (2): 179-191; Arturo Escobar and Sonia E. Alvarez, eds., 1992, *The Making of Social Movements in Latin America: Identity, Strategy, and Democracy* (Boulder, Colo.: Westview Press); Rodolfo Stavenhagen, 1996, *Ethnic Conflicts and the Nation-state* (New York: St. Martin's Press); and Enrique Larana, Hank Johnston, and Joseph R. Gusfield, eds., 1994, *New Social Movements: From Ideology to Identity* (Philadelphia: Temple University Press).

117. For a parallel analysis, see Manuel A. Garretón, 1996, "Social Movements and the Process of Democratization: A General Framework" *International Review of Sociology* 6 (1).

118. See Gary Gereffi, Ronie Garcia-Johnson, and Erika Sasser, 2001, "The NGO-Industrial Complex" *Foreign Policy* (July-August): 56-65.

119. For discussions, see Héctor Díaz Polanco, 1997, *Indigenous Peoples in Latin America: The Quest for Self-Determination* (Boulder, Colo.: Westview Press). Also, Lynne Phillips, ed., 1998, *The Third Wave of Modernization in Latin America: Cultural Perspectives on Neoliberalism* (Washington, D.C.: Scholarly Resources).

120. An example, ultimately, of the latter is the Zapatista movement in the state of Chiapas, Mexico; see Tom Hayden, ed., 2002, *The Zapatista Reader* (New York: Thunder's Mouth Press, Nation Books); and Carlos Montemayor, 1998, *Chiapas, la rebelión indígena de México* (Madrid: Espasa Calpe).

REFERENCES

Aguilar Zinser, Adolfo. 2001. "Mexico's Security Challenges." *Update on the Americas.* No. 2: December. Washington, D.C.: Woodrow Wilson Center.

Agüero, Felipe, and Jeffrey Stark, eds. 1998. *Fault Lines of Democracy in Post-Transition Latin America.* Coral Gables, Fla: North-South Center Press at the University of Miami.

Alcántara Sáez, Manuel. 1994. *Gobernabilidad, crisis y cambio: elementos para el estudio de la gobernabilidad de los sistemas políticos en épocas de crisis y cambio.* Madrid: Centro de Estudios Constitucionales.

Alcántara Sáez, Manuel, and Ismael Crespo, eds. 1995. *Los Límites de la Consolidación Democrática en América Latina.* Salamanca, Spain: Ediciones Universidad de Salamanca.

Alvarez, Sonia E., Evelina Dagnino, and Arturo Escobar, eds. 1998. *Cultures of Politics/Politics of Cultures: Revisioning Latin American Social Movements.* Boulder, Colo.: Westview Press.

Appadurai, Arjun. 1996. *Modernity at Large: Cultural Dimensions of Globalization.* Minneapolis: University of Minnesota Press.

Avritzer, Leonardo, ed. 1994. *Sociedade Civil e Democratização.* Belo Horizonte: Livraria del Rey Editora.

Bagley, Bruce M., and William O. Walker III, eds. 1994. *Drug Trafficking in the Americas.* Coral Gables, Fla: North-South Center Press at the University of Miami.

Ballén, Rafael. 1994. *Corrupción Política.* Bogotá: Ediciones Acropolis.

Barba Solano, Carlos, José Luis Barros, and Javier Hurtado, eds. 1991. *Transiciones a la Democracia en Europa y América Latina.* Mexico City: M.A. Porrua Grupo Editorial.

Barbero, Jesús Martín. 1993. Translated by Elizabeth Fox and Robert A. White. *Communication, Culture and Hegemony: From the Media to Mediations.* London: Sage Publications, Inc.

Barbero, Jesús Martín, Fabio López de la Roche, Jaime Eduardo Jaramillo and Renato Ortiz, eds. 1999. *Cultura y globalización.* Bogotá: Universidad Nacional de Colombia, Centro de Estudios Sociales.

Barros, José Luis, Javier Hurtado, and German Pérez Fernandez del Castillo, eds. 1991. *Transición a la Democracia y Reforma del Estado en México.* Mexico City: M.A. Porrua Grupo Editorial.

Bejarano, Ana María, and Eduardo Pizarro. 2001. "Reforma política después de 1991: ¿Qué queda por reformar?" Paper presented to a conference at the Helen Kellogg Institute for International Studies, University of Notre Dame, March.

119

Bello, Walden F. 1994. *Dark Victory: The United States, Structural Adjustment, and Global Poverty.* London: Pluto Press.

Bermeo, Nancy. 1992. "Democracy and the Lessons of Dictatorship." *Comparative Politics* 23 (3): 273-292.

Berry, Albert, ed. 1998. *Poverty, Economic Reform, and Income Distribution in Latin America.* Boulder, Colo.: Lynne Rienner Publishers.

Bethell, Leslie, ed. 1994. *Cambridge History of Latin America* Vol. VI, part I. Cambridge, UK: Cambridge University Press.

Birch, Melissa H., and Jerry Haar, eds. 1999. *The Impact of Privatization in Latin America.* Coral Gables, Fla: North-South Center Press at the University of Miami.

Bizzozer, Lincoln, and Marcel Vaillant, eds. 1996. *La Inserción Internacional del MERCOSUR: Mirando al Sur o Mirando al Norte?* Montevideo: Arca.

Borón, Atilio. 1995. *State, Capitalism, and Democracy in Latin America.* Boulder, Colo.: Lynne Rienner Publishers.

Bouzas, Roberto, and Jaime Ros, eds. 1994. *Economic Integration in the Western Hemisphere.* Notre Dame, Ind.: University of Notre Dame Press.

Bradford, Colin I., ed. 1994. *Redefining the State in Latin America.* Paris: Organization for Economic Cooperation and Development.

Buitelaar, Ruud, and Pitou van Dijck. 1996. *Latin America's Insertion in the World Economy: Towards Systemic Competitiveness in Small Economies.* New York: St. Martin's Press.

Cammack, Paul. 1994. "Democratization and Citizenship in Latin America." In *Democracy and Democratization,* eds. Geraint Parry and Michael Moran. London: Routledge.

Cardoso, Fernando Henrique, and Enzo Faletto. 1979. *Dependency and Development in Latin America.* Berkeley, Calif.: University of California Press.

Carnoy, Martin, Manuel Castells, Stephen S. Cohen, and Fernando Henrique Cardoso. 1993. *The New Global Economy in the Information Age: Reflections on a Changing World.* University Park, Pa.: Pennsylvania State University Press.

Casper, Gretchen, and Michelle M. Taylor, eds. 1996. *Negotiating Democracy: Transitions from Authoritarian Rule.* Pittsburgh: University of Pittsburgh Press.

Cavarozzi, Marcelo. 1982. "El 'desarrollismo' y las relaciones entre democracia y capitalismo dependiente en 'Dependencia y desarrollo en América Latina.'" *Latin American Research Review* 17 (3): 166-171.

Cavarozzi, Marcelo. 1986. "Peronism and Radicalism: Argentina's Transition in Perspective." In *Elections and Democratization in Latin America, 1980-1985,* eds. Paul W. Drake and Eduardo Silva. La Jolla, Calif.: Center for Iberian and Latin American Studies, University of California.

Cavarozzi, Marcelo. 1992. "Beyond Transitions to Democracy in Latin America." *Journal of Latin American Studies* 24 (3): 65-84.

Cavarozzi, Marcelo. 1994. "Politics: A Key for the Long Term in South America." In *Latin American Political Economy in the Age of Neoliberal Reform: Theoretical and Comparative Perspectives for the 1990s*, eds. William C. Smith, Carlos H. Acuña, and Eduardo A. Gamarra. Coral Gables, Fla: North-South Center Press at the University of Miami.

Cavarozzi, Marcelo. 1995. "Los partidos políticos latinoamericanos, sus configuraciones históricas y su papel en las transiciones recientes." In *Los Límites de la Consolidación Democrática en América Latina*, eds. Manuel Alcántara and Ismael Crespo. Salamanca, Spain: Ediciones Universidad de Salamanca.

Cavarozzi, Marcelo, and Manuel Antonio Garretón, eds. 1989. *Muerte y Resurrección: Los Partidos Políticos en el Autoritarismo y las Transiciones en el Cono Sur*. Santiago: FLACSO.

Cavarozzi, Marcelo, and Juan Abel Medina, eds. 2002. *El asedio a la política: Los partidos latinoamericanos en la era neoliberal*. Buenos Aires: Editorial Politeia.

CEPAL (Comisión Económica para América Latina y el Caribe). 1992. *Equidad y Transformación Productiva: Un Enfoque Integrado*. Santiago: CEPAL.

CEPAL. 2001. *Panorama Social de América Latina, 2000-2001*. Santiago: CEPAL.

Chalmers, Douglas A., Carlos M. Vilas, Katherine Hite, Scott B. Martin, Kerianne Piester, and Monique Segura, eds. 1997. *The New Politics of Inequality in Latin America: Rethinking Participation and Representation*. Oxford: Oxford University Press.

Chonchol, Jacques. 2000. *Hacia dónde nos lleva la globalización?* Santiago: LOM Ediciones.

Cleaves, Peter S. 1974. *Bureaucratic Politics and Administration in Chile*. Berkeley, Calif.: University of California Press.

Cleaves, Peter S. 1987. *The Professions and the State: The Mexican Case*. Tucson: University of Arizona Press.

Cleaves, Peter S. 1995. "Empresarios y política empresarial en América Latina." In *Los Límites a la Consolidación Democrática en América Latina*, eds. Manuel Alcántara Sáez and Ismael Crespo. Salamanca, Spain: Ediciones Universidad de Salamanca.

Cohen, Jean L. 1983. "Rethinking Social Movements." *Berkeley Journal of Sociology* 28: 97-114.

Collier, David, and Ruth Berins. 1991. *Shaping the Political Arena: Critical Junctures, the Labor Movement, and Regime Dynamics in Latin America*. Princeton, N.J.: Princeton University Press.

Collier, David, and Steven Levitsky. 1997. "Democracy with 'Adjectives.'" *World Politics* 49 (3): 430-452.

Canclini, Néstor García. 1999. *La globalización imaginada*. México, D.F.: Fondo de Cultura Económica.

Coppedge, Michael. 1998. "The Evolution of Latin American Party Systems." In *Politics, Society, and Democracy: Latin America,* eds. Scott Mainwaring and Arturo Valenzuela. Boulder, Colo.: Westview Press.

CORDES (Corporación de Estudios para el Desarrollo). 1987. *Neoliberalismo y Políticas Económicas Alternativas.* Quito, Ecuador: CORDES.

Corradi, José E., Patricia Weiss Fagen, and Manuel Antonio Garretón, eds. 1992. *Fear at the Edge: State Terror and Resistance in Latin America.* Berkeley, Calif.: University of California Press.

Dahl, Robert A. 1971. *Polyarchy: Participation and Opposition.* New Haven, Conn.: Yale University Press.

Devlin, Robert. 1989. *Debt and Crisis in Latin America: The Supply Side of the Story.* Princeton, N.J.: Princeton University Press.

Diamond, Larry. 1999. *Developing Democracy: Toward Consolidation.* Baltimore: The Johns Hopkins University Press.

Diamond, Larry, Jonathan Hartlyn, Juan J. Linz, and Seymour Martin Lipset, eds. 1999. *Democracy in Developing Countries: Latin America*, 2nd ed., Boulder, Colo.: Lynne Rienner Publishers.

Diamond, Larry, Jonathan Hartlyn, and Juan J. Linz. 1999. "Introduction: Politics, Society, and Democracy in Latin America." In *Democracy in Developing Countries: Latin America*, 2nd ed., eds. Larry Diamond, Jonathan Hartlyn, Juan J. Linz and Seymour Martin Lipset. Boulder, Colo.: Lynne Rienner Publishers.

Díaz Polanco, Héctor. 1997. *Indigenous Peoples in Latin America: The Quest for Self-Determination.* Boulder, Colo.: Westview Press.

Díaz-Alejandro, Carlos. 1980 (March). *Latin America in Depression.* Discussion Paper No. 344. New Haven, Conn.: Yale University Economic Growth Center.

Díaz-Alejandro, Carlos. 1981 (April). *Some Lessons of the 1930s for the 1980s.* Discussion Paper No. 376. New Haven, Conn.: Yale University Economic Growth Center.

Dicken, Peter. 1982. *Transforming the World Economy.* 3rd ed. New York: Guilford Publications.

Dicken, Peter. 1998. *Global Shift: Transforming the World Economy.* 3rd ed. New York: Guilford Publications.

Dietz, James L., ed. 1995. *Latin America's Economic Development: Confronting Crisis.* Boulder, Colo.: Lynne Rienner Publishers.

Dornbusch, Rudiger. 1991. "Structural Adjustment in Latin America." Latin American Program Working Paper No.191. Washington, D.C.: The Woodrow Wilson Center for Scholars.

Dos Santos, Mario. 1994. *Estratégias de gobernabilidad en la crisis.* Project Report RLA 90/011 (June). United Nations Development Programme-United Nations Educational, Scientific, and Cultural Organization-Consejo Latinoamericano de Ciencias Sociales (UNDP-UNESCO-CLACSO).

Drake, Paul W., and Eduardo Silva, eds. 1986. *Elections and Democratization in Latin America, 1980-1985*. La Jolla, Calif.: Center for Iberian and Latin American Studies, University of California.

Durand, Francisco, and Eduardo Silva, eds. 1998. *Organized Business, Economic Change, and Democracy in Latin America*. Coral Gables, Fla: North-South Center Press at the University of Miami.

Eade, John, ed. 1997. *Living the Global City: Globalization as a Local Process*. New York: Routledge.

Eckstein, Susan, ed. 2001. *Power and Popular Protest: Latin American Social Movements*. Berkeley, Calif.: University of California Press.

The Economist. 1997. "The World Economy Survey." September (20).

Edwards, Sebastian. 1995. *Crisis and Reform in Latin America: From Despair to Hope*. Oxford, UK: Oxford University Press.

Escobar, Arturo, and Sonia E. Alvarez, eds. 1992. *The Making of Social Movements in Latin America: Identity, Strategy, and Democracy*. Boulder, Colo.: Westview Press.

Esping-Andersen, Gøsta. 1990. *The Three Worlds of Welfare Capitalism*. Princeton, N.J.: Princeton University Press.

Evans, Peter B., Dietrich Rueschemeyer, and Theda Skocpol, eds. 1985. *Bringing the State Back In*. Cambridge, UK: Cambridge University Press.

Fajnzylber, Fernando. 1990. *Unavoidable Industrial Restructuring in Latin America*. Durham, N.C.: Duke University Press.

Fanelli, José María, Roberto Frenkel, and Guillermo Rozenwurcel. 1990. *Growth and Structural Reform in Latin America. Where Do We Stand?* Buenos Aires: Centro de Estudios del Estado y Sociedad (CEDES).

Featherstone, Mike. 1996. *Undoing Culture: The Globalization of Capitalism in Third World Countries*. Westport, Conn.: Praeger Publishers.

Ffrench-Davis, Ricardo. 1999. *Macroeconomía, comercio y finanzas: Para reformar las reformas en América Latina*. Santiago: McGraw-Hill.

Ffrench-Davis, Ricardo, and Stephany Griffith-Jones, eds. 1995. *Coping with Capital Surges: The Return of Finance to Latin America*. Boulder, Colo.: Lynne Rienner Publishers.

Ffrench-Davis, Ricardo, ed. 1999. *Entre el Neoliberalismo y el crecimiento con equidad*. Santiago: Dolmen Ediciones.

Filgueira, Carlos H. 2001. *La actualidad de viejas temáticas: sobre los estudios de clase, estratificación y movilidad en América Latina*. Santiago: CEPAL.

Filgueira, Carlos H., and Dieter Nohlen, eds. 1994. *Prensa y Transición Democrática: Experiencias Recientes en Europa y América Latina*. Frankfurt: Vervuert.

Fishlow, Albert. 1985. "Lessons from the Past: Capital Markets during the 19th Century and the Interwar Period." *International Organization* 39 (3).

Fitch, J. Samuel. 1991. "Democracy, Human Rights, and the Armed Forces in Latin America." In *The United States and Latin America in the 1990s: Beyond the Cold War*, eds. Jonathan Hartlyn, Lars Schoultz, and Augusto Varas. Chapel Hill, N.C.: University of North Carolina Press.

Flores Díaz, Max, Adicea Castillo, Antonio Montilla, Hector Silva Michelena, and Haleis Davila. *La Industrialización y Desarrollo en América Latina.* Caracas: Universidad Central de Venezuela, Facultad de Ciencias Económicas y Sociales, Instituto de Investigaciones Económicas y Sociales.

Follain, John. 1998. *Jackal: The Secret Wars of Carlos the Jackal.* London: Weidenfeld & Nicolson.

Fox, Elizabeth, ed. 1988. *Media and Politics in Latin America: The Struggle for Democracy.* Newbury Park, Calif.: Sage Publications, Inc.

Fuentes, Marta, and André Gunder Frank. 1989. "Ten Theses on Social Movements." *World Development* 17 (2): 179-191.

Garcia Canclini, Nestor. 1995. *Hybrid Cultures: Strategies for Entering and Leaving Modernity.* Translated by Christopher L. Chiappari and Silvia L. López. Minneapolis: University of Minnesota Press.

Garretón, Manuel A. 1984. *Dictaduras y Democratización.* Santiago de Chile: Facultad Latinoamericana de Ciencias Sociales (FLACSO).

Garretón, Manuel A. 1987. *Reconstruir la Política.* Santiago de Chile: Editorial Andante.

Garretón, Manuel A. 1988. *The Chilean Political Process.* Boston: Unwin Hyman.

Garretón, Manuel A. 1989. *Las Transiciones a la Democracia y el Caso Chileno.* Discussion Paper No. 116. Santiago de Chile: FLACSO.

Garretón, Manuel Antonio. 1991. "Política, cultura y sociedad en la Transición Democrática." *Nueva Sociedad* No. 114 (July-August). Caracas.

Garretón, Manuel Antonio. 1995a. "Democracia, modernización, desarrollo: Hacia una nueva problemática en América Latina." In *Dimensiones actuales de la sociología*, eds. Manuel Antonio Garretón and Orlando Mella. Santiago: Bravo y Allende.

Garretón, Manuel A. 1995b. *Hacia una Nueva Era Política: Estudio sobre las Democratizaciones.* Mexico City: Fondo de Cultura Económica.

Garretón, Manuel A. 1996. "Social Movements and the Process of Democratization: A General Framework." *International Review of Sociology* 6 (1).

Garretón, Manuel A. 1999. *Política y sociedad entre dos épocas. América Latina en el cambio de siglo.* Buenos Aires: Homo Sapiens.

Garretón, Manuel A., ed. 1999. *América Latina: un espacio cultural en el mundo globalizado, debates y perspectives.* Santafé de Bogotá: Convenio Andrés Bello.

Garretón, Manuel A. 2000. *La sociedad en que vivi(re)mos. Introducción sociológica al cambio de siglo.* Santiago: LOM Ediciones.

Garretón, Manuel A. 2002. "The New Sociopolitical Matrix." In *(Re)constructing Political Society*, eds., M.A. Garretón and E. Newman. Tokyo: United Nations University Press.

Garretón, Manuel Antonio. 2002. "La transformación de la acción colectiva en América Latina." *Revista de la CEPAL* 76 (April): 7-24.

Garretón, Manuel Antonio, and Malva Espinosa. 1992. *¿Reforma del Estado o Cambios en la Matriz Socio-política?* Programa Chile. Santiago de Chile: FLACSO.

Garretón, Manuel Antonio, and Orlando Mella, eds. 1995. *Dimensiones actuales de la sociología.* Santiago: Bravo y Allende.

Gereffi, Gary. 1995. "Global Production Systems and Third World Development." In *Global Change, Regional Response: The New International Context of Development*, ed. Barbara Stallings. Cambridge, UK: Cambridge University Press.

Gereffi, Gary. 2001. "Shifting Governance Structures in Global Commodity Chains, with Special Reference to the Internet." *American Behavioral Scientist* 44 (10): 1616-1637.

Gereffi, Gary. 2003. "Mexico's Industrial Development: Climbing Ahead or Falling Behind in the World Economy?" In *Confronting Development: Assessing Mexico's Economic and Social Policy Changes*, eds. Kevin Middlebrook and Eduardo Zepeda. Stanford, Calif.: Stanford University Press.

Gereffi, Gary, and Lynn Hempel. 1996. "Latin America in the Global Economy: Running Faster to Stay in Place." *NACLA — Report on the Americas* 29 (4).

Gereffi, Gary, Ronie Garcia-Johnson, and Erika Sasser. 2001. "The NGO-Industrial Complex." *Foreign Policy* (July-August): 56-65.

Gereffi, Gary, and Miguel Korzeniewicz. 1994. *Commodity Chains and Global Capitalism.* Westport, Conn.: Praeger Publishers.

Gereffi, Gary, and Donald Wyman, eds. 1990. *Manufacturing Miracles: Paths of Industrialization in Latin America and East Asia.* Princeton, N.J.: Princeton University Press.

Gereffi, Gary, David Spener, and Jennifer Bair, eds. 2002. *Free Trade and Uneven Development: The North American Apparel Industry After NAFTA.* Philadelphia, Pa: Temple University Press.

Germani, Gino. 1978. *Authoritarianism, Fascism, and National Populism.* New Brusnwick, N.J.: Transaction Books.

Glade, William P., and Rossana Corona, eds. 1996. *Bigger Economies, Smaller Governments: Privatization in Latin America.* Boulder, Colo.: Westview Press.

Graciarena, Jorge. 1967. *Poder y Clases Sociales en el Desarrollo de América Latina.* Buenos Aires: Paidos.

Griffith-Jones, Stephany. 1984. *International Finance and Latin America.* London: Croom Helm.

Griffith-Jones, Stephany, and Barbara Stallings. 1995. "New Global Financial Trends: Implications for Development." In *Global Change, Regional Response: The New International Context of Development*, ed. Barbara Stallings. Cambridge, UK: Cambridge University Press.

Hardt, Michael, and Antonio Negri. 2000. *Empire.* Cambridge, Mass.: Harvard University Press.

Harnecker, Marta. 1978. *Los conceptos elementales del materialismo histórico.* México, D.F.: Siglo Veintiuno Editores.

Harris, Nigel. 1987. *The End of the Third World.* New York: Penguin Books.

Hartlyn, Jonathan, and Arturo Valenzuela. 1994. "Democracy in Latin America since 1930." In *Cambridge History of Latin America* Vol. VI: Part II, ed. Leslie Bethell. Cambridge, UK: Cambridge University Press.

Hartlyn, Jonathan. 1997. "Democracy in South America: Convergences and Diversities." In *Argentina: The Challenges of Modernization,* eds. Joseph S. Tulchin and Allison Garland. Wilmington, Del.: Scholarly Resources, Inc.

Hartlyn, Jonathan. 2001. "Constitutional Powers: Legislative Power and Its Relation to Executive Power." Paper presented at the Conference on Democratic Transition and Consolidation. Madrid, October 18-20.

Hartlyn, Jonathan. 2002. "Democracy and Consolidation in Contemporary Latin America: Current Thinking and Future Challenges." In *Democratic Governance and Social Inequality,* ed. Joseph Tulchin. Boulder, Colo.: Lynne Rienner Publishers.

Hartlyn, Jonathan, and John Dugas. 1999. "Colombia: The Politics of Violence and Democratic Transformation." In *Democracy in Developing Countries: Latin America,* 2nd ed., eds. Larry Diamond, Jonathan Hartlyn, Juan J. Linz, and Seymour Martin Lipset. Boulder, Colo.: Lynne Rienner Publishers.

Hartlyn, Jonathan, Lars Schoultz, and Augusto Varas, eds. 1991. *The United States and Latin America in the 1990s: Beyond the Cold War.* Chapel Hill, N.C.: University of North Carolina Press.

Hayden, Tom, ed. 2002. *The Zapatista Reader.* New York: Thunder's Mouth Press, Nation Books.

Helleiner, Eric. 1994. *States and the Reemergence of Global Finance: From Bretton Woods to the 1990s.* Ithaca, N.Y.: Cornell University Press.

Heper, Metin. 1991. "Transitions to Democracy Reconsidered." In *Comparative Political Dynamics,* eds. Dankwart A. Rustow and Kenneth Paul Erickson. New York: HarperCollins.

Higley John, and Richard Gunther, eds. 1992. *Elites and Democratic Consolidation in Latin America and Southern Europe.* New York: Cambridge University Press.

Hirschman, Alberto O. 1971. *A Bias for Hope: Essays on Development and Latin America.* New Haven, Conn.: Yale University Press.

Hirst, Paul Q. 1996. *Globalization in Question: The International Political Economy and the Possibilities of Governance.* Cambridge, UK: Polity Press.

Hopenhayn, Martín. 2001. *No Apocalypse, No Integration: Modernism and Postmodernism in Latin America.* Translated by Cynthia Margarita Tompkins and Elizabeth Rosa Horan. Durham, N.C.: Duke University Press.

Huber, Evelyne. 1995. *Options for Social Policy in Latin America: Neo-Liberal versus Social Democratic Models.* Discussion Paper 66 (June). Geneva: United Nations Research Institute for Social Development.

Huber, Evelyne, and John D. Stephens. 2001. *Development and Crisis of the Welfare State: Parties and Policies in Global Markets.* Chicago: University of Chicago Press.

Huber, Evelyne, and Michelle Dion. 2002. "Revolution or Contribution? Rational Choice Approaches in the Study of Latin American Politics." *Latin American Politics and Society* 44 (3): 1-28.

Hunter, Wendy. 1996. *State and Soldier in Latin America: Redefining the Military's Role in Argentina, Brazil, and Chile.* Peaceworks No. 10. Washington, D.C.: United States Institute of Peace.

Hunter, Wendy. 1997. *Eroding Military Influence in Brazil: Politicians Against Soldiers.* Chapel Hill, N.C.: University of North Carolina Press.

Huntington, Samuel P. 1968. *Political Order in Changing Societies.* New Haven, Conn.: Yale University Press.

Huntington, Samuel P. 1984. "Will More Countries Become Democratic?" *Political Science Quarterly* 99 (Summer): 193-218.

Huntington, Samuel P. 1991. *The Third Wave: Democratization in the Late Twentieth Century.* Norman, Okla.: University of Oklahoma Press.

Inter-American Democratic Charter. <http://www.oas.org/charter/docs/resolution1_en _p4.htm>.

Inter-American Development Bank (IDB). 1993. *Social Reform and Poverty: Toward a Comprehensive Agenda for Development.* Washington, D.C.: Forum on Social Reform and Poverty, IDB.

Inter-American Development Bank. 1998. *Facing Up to Inequality in Latin America: Economic and Social Progress in Latin America 1998-1999.* Report. Washington, D.C.: IDB, distributed by The Johns Hopkins University Press.

Inter-American Development Bank. 2000. *Development Beyond Economics: Economic and Social Progress in Latin America 2000 Report.* Washington, D.C.: IDB, distributed by The Johns Hopkins University Press.

International Monetary Fund (IMF). 2002. *World Economic Outlook.* (September).

Jelin, Elizabeth, and Eric Hershberg, eds. 1996. *Constructing Democracy: Human Rights, Citizenship, and Society in Latin America.* Boulder, Colo.: Westview Press.

Johnson, Hazel J. 1993. *Financial Institutions and Markets: A Global Perspective.* New York: McGraw-Hill.

Joyce, Elizabeth, and Carlos Malamud, eds. 1997. *Latin America and the Multinational Drug Trade.* New York: St. Martin's Press.

Kapstein, Ethan B. 1994. *Governing the Global Economy: International Finance and the State.* Cambridge, Mass.: Harvard University Press.

Karl, Terry Lynn. 1990. "Dilemmas of Democratization in Latin America." *Comparative Politics* 23 (1): 1-21.

Kashiwagi, Yusuke. 1986. *The Emergence of Global Finance.* Washington, D.C.: Per Jacobsson Foundation.

Katz, Jorge M., ed. 1987. *Technology Generation in Latin American Manufacturing Industries.* New York: St. Martin's Press.

Keck, Margaret, and Kathryn Sikkink. 1998. *Activists Beyond Borders: Advocacy Networks in International Politics.* Ithaca, N.Y.: Cornell University Press.

Kleymeyer, Charles David, ed. 1994. *Cultural Expression and Grassroots Development: Cases from Latin America and the Caribbean.* Boulder, Colo.: Lynne Rienner Publishers.

Kliksberg, Bernardo. 1997. *Como Enfrentar los Déficits Sociales de América Latina.* San José, Costa Rica: FLACSO.

Klitgaard, Robert E. 1988. *Controlling Corruption.* Berkeley, Calif.: University of California Press.

Lanz, Rigoberto, ed. 1993. *La Discusión Posmoderna.* Caracas: Fondo Editorial Tropykos.

Larana, Enrique, Hank Johnston, and Joseph R. Gusfield, eds. 1994. *New Social Movements: From Ideology to Identity.* Philadelphia: Temple University Press.

Lardner, James. 1988. "The Sweater Trade — I." *The New Yorker*, January 11: 39-73.

Larraín, Jorge. 1996. *Modernidad, Razón e Identidad en América Latina.* Santiago: Editorial Andrés Bello.

Levine, Daniel H., ed. 1993. *Constructing Culture and Power in Latin America.* Ann Arbor, Mich.: University of Michigan Press.

Levy, Daniel, and Kathleen Bruhn. 1999. "Mexico: Sustained Civilian Rule and the Question of Democracy." In *Democracy in Developing Countries: Latin America*, 2nd ed., eds. Larry Diamond, Jonathan Hartlyn, Juan J. Linz, and Seymour Martin Lipset. Boulder, Colo.: Lynne Rienner Publishers.

Linz, Juan J. 1973. "The Future of an Authoritarian Situation or the Institutionalization of an Authoritarian Regime: The Case of Brazil." In *Authoritarian Brazil: Origins, Policies, and Future*, ed. Alfred Stepan. New Haven, Conn.: Yale University Press.

Linz, Juan J. 1996. "Toward Consolidated Democracies." *Journal of Democracy* 7 (2): 14-34.

Linz, Juan J., Arend Lijphart, Arturo Valenzuela, and Oscar Godoy Arcaya, eds. 1990. *Hacia una Democracia Moderna: La Opción Parlamentaria.* Santiago: Ediciones Universidad Católica de Chile.

Linz, Juan J., and Alfred Stepan. 1996. *Problems of Democratic Transition and Consolidation: Southern Europe, South America, and Post-Communist Europe.* Baltimore: The Johns Hopkins University Press.

Linz, Juan J., and Arturo Valenzuela, eds. 1994. *The Failure of Presidential Democracy.* Baltimore: The Johns Hopkins University Press.

Little, Walter, and Eduardo Posada-Carbó, eds. 1996. *Political Corruption in Latin America and Europe.* New York: St. Martin's Press.

Lorey, David E. 1992. *The Rise of the Professions in Twentieth-Century Mexico: University Graduates and Occupational Change since 1929.* Los Angeles: UCLA Latin American Center Publications.

Love, Joseph L. 1994. "Economic Ideas and Ideologies in Latin America since 1930." In *Cambridge History of Latin America.* Vol. VI, part I, ed. Leslie Bethell. Cambridge, UK: Cambridge University Press.

Loveman, Brian, and Thomas M. Davies, Jr., eds. 1996. *The Politics of Antipolitics: The Military in Latin America,* 3rd ed. Washington, D.C.: Scholarly Resources.

Lowenthal, Abraham F., ed. 1991. *Exporting Democracy: The United States and Latin America.* Baltimore: The Johns Hopkins University Press.

Lowenthal, Abraham F., and J. Samuel Fitch, eds. 1986. *Armies and Politics in Latin America.* New York: Holmes and Meier.

Luebbert, Gregory. 1991. *Liberalism, Fascism, or Social Democracy: Social Classes and Political Origins of Regimes in Interwar Europe.* Oxford, UK: Oxford University Press.

Lustig, Nora, ed. 1995. *Coping with Austerity: Poverty and Inequality in Latin America.* Washington, D.C.: The Brookings Institution.

Mace, Gordon, and Louis Bélanger, eds. 1999. *The Americas in Transition: The Contours of Regionalism.* Boulder, Colo.: Lynne Rienner Publishers.

Mainwaring, Scott P. 1987. "Urban Popular Movements, Identity, and Democratization in Brazil." *Comparative Political Studies* 20 (2): 131-159.

Mainwaring, Scott P. 1999. *Rethinking Party Systems in the Third Wave of Democratization: The Case of Brazil.* Stanford, Calif.: Stanford University Press.

Mainwaring, Scott P., Guillermo O'Donnell, and J. Samuel Valenzuela, eds. 1992. *Issues in Democratic Consolidation: The New South American Democracies in Comparative Perspective.* Notre Dame, Ind.: University of Notre Dame Press.

Mainwaring, Scott P., and Timothy Scully, eds. 1995. *Building Democratic Institutions: Party Systems in Latin America.* Stanford, Calif.: Stanford University Press.

Mainwaring, Scott P., and Matthew Shugart. 1997a. "Juan Linz, Presidentialism, and Democracy: A Critical Appraisal." *Comparative Politics* (July): 449-471.

Mainwaring, Scott P., and Matthew Shugart, eds. 1997b. *Presidentialism and Democracy in Latin America.* Cambridge, UK: Cambridge University Press.

Mainwaring, Scott P., and Arturo Valenzuela, eds. 1998. *Politics, Society, and Democracy: Latin America.* Boulder, Colo.: Westview Press.

Mainwaring, Scott P., and Eduardo Viola. 1984. "New Social Movements, Political Culture, and Democracy: Brazil and Argentina in the 1980s." *Telos* No. 61 (Fall): 17-54.

Manzetti, Luigi. 1994. "Latin America: Privatization, Property Rights, and Deregulation." *Quarterly Review of Economics and Finance Annual* 34: 43-77.

Martínez, Javier, and Alvaro Díaz. 1996. *Chile: The Great Transformation.* Washington, D.C.: The Brookings Institution and the UN Research Institute for Social Development.

McAnany, Emile G., and Kenton T. Wilkinson, eds. 1996. *Mass Media and Free Trade: NAFTA and the Cultural Industries.* Austin, Texas: University of Texas Press.

McGuire, James. 1997. *Peronism without Perón: Unions, Parties, and Democracy in Argentina.* Stanford, Calif.: Stanford University Press.

Mayer, Frederick W. 1998. *Interpreting NAFTA: The Science and Art of Political Analysis.* New York: Columbia University.

Meneguello, Rachel. 2002. "Brasil." In *El asedio a la política: Los partidos latinoamericanos en la era neoliberal*, eds. Marcelo Cavarozzi and Juan Abel Medina. Buenos Aires: Editorial Politeia.

Méndez, Juan E., Guillermo O'Donnell, and Paulo Sérgio Pinheiro, eds. 1999. *The Rule of Law and the Underprivileged in Latin America.* Notre Dame, Ind.: University of Notre Dame Press.

Middlebrook, Kevin, and Eduardo Zepeda, eds. 2003. *Confronting Development: Assessing Mexico's Economic and Social Policy Changes.* Stanford, Calif.: Stanford University Press.

Millett, Richard L., and Michael Gold-Biss, eds. 1996. *Beyond Praetorianism: The Latin American Military in Transition.* Coral Gables, Fla: North-South Center Press at the University of Miami.

Milner, Helen. 1997. *Interests, Institutions, and Information.* Princeton, N.J.: Princeton University Press.

Misztal, Bronislaw, and Barbara A. Misztal. 1988. "Democratization Processes as an Objective of New Social Movements." *Research in Social Movements, Conflicts and Change* 10: 93-106.

Montemayor, Carlos. 1998. *Chiapas, la rebelión indígena de México.* Madrid: Espasa Calpe.

Montgomery, Tommie Sue, ed. 2000. *Peacemaking and Democratization in the Western Hemisphere.* Coral Gables, Fla: North-South Center Press at the University of Miami.

Morales, Juan Antonio, and Gary McMahon, eds. 1996. *Economic Policy and the Transition to Democracy: The Latin American Experience.* New York: St. Martin's Press.

Morris, Stephen D. 1991. *Corruption and Politics in Contemporary Mexico.* Tuscaloosa, Ala.: University of Alabama Press.

Moulián, Tomás. 1984. *Tensiones y Crisis Política: Análisis de la Década del Sesenta.* Santiago: Centro de Estudios para el Desarrollo (CED).

Munck, Gerardo. 2001. "Game Theory and Comparative Politics." *World Politics* 53 (2): 173-204.

Nohlen, Dieter, ed. 1993. *Elecciones y Sistemas de Partidos en América Latina*. San José, Costa Rica: Instituto Interamericano de Derechos Humanos.

Nohlen, Dieter, and Mario Fernández, eds. 1991. *Presidencialismo versus Parlamentarismo, América Latina*. Caracas: Editorial Nueva Sociedad.

Nunn, Frederick M. 1976. *The Military in Chilean History: Essays on Civil-Military Relations, 1810-1973*. Albuquerque, N.M.: University of New Mexico Press.

Nunn, Frederick M. 1992. *The Time of the Generals: Latin American Professional Militarism in World Perspective*. Lincoln, Neb.: University of Nebraska Press.

O'Donnell, Guillermo, Philippe C. Schmitter, and Laurence Whitehead. 1986. *Transitions from Authoritarian Rule: Tentative Conclusions about Uncertain Democracies*. Baltimore: The Johns Hopkins University Press.

O'Donnell, Guillermo. 1994a. "Delegative Democracy." *Journal of Democracy* 5 (1): 55-69.

O'Donnell, Guillermo. 1994b. "Some Reflections on Redefining the Role of the State." In *Redefining the State in Latin America*, ed. Colin I. Bradford. Paris: Organization for Economic Cooperation and Development (OECD).

Olea, Víctor Flores, and Abelardo Mariña Flores. 1999. *Crítica de la globalidad: Dominación y liberación en nuestro tiempo*. México, D.F.: Fondo de Cultura Económica.

Oliveri, Ernest J. 1992. *Latin American Debt and the Politics of International Finance*. Westport, Conn.: Praeger Publishers.

Organization of American States (OAS) Resolution 1080. <http://www.oas.org/ Assembly2001/assembly/GAAssembly2000/resolucion1080.htm>.

Oxhorn, Philip. 1995. *Organizing Civil Society: The Popular Sectors and the Struggle for Democracy in Chile*. University Park, Pa.: Pennsylvania State University Press.

Oxhorn, Philip, and Pamela K. Starr, eds. 1998. *Markets and Democracy in Latin America: Conflict or Convergence?* Boulder, Colo.: Lynne Rienner Publishers.

Parry, Geraint, and Michael Moran, eds. 1994. *Democracy and Democratization*. London: Routledge.

Pattnayak, Satya R., ed. 1996. *Globalization, Urbanization, and the State: Selected Studies in Contemporary Latin America*. Lanham, Md.: University Press of America.

Payne, Mark J., Daniel G. Zovatto, Fernando Carrillo Flórez, and Andrés Allamand Zavala. 2002. *Democracies in Development: Politics and Reform in Latin America*. Washington, D.C.: IDB and IDEA.

Peters, Enrique Dussel. 2000. *Polarizing Mexico: The Impact of Liberalization Strategy*. Boulder, Colo.: Lynne Rienner Publishers.

Pérez Díaz, Víctor. 1993. *La Primacia de la Sociedad Civil: El Proceso de Formación de la España Democrática*. Madrid: Alianza Editorial.

Phillips, Lynne, ed. 1998. *The Third Wave of Modernization in Latin America: Cultural Perspectives on Neoliberalism.* Washington, D.C.: Scholarly Resources.

Pion-Berlin, David. 1997. *Through Corridors of Power: Institutions and Civil-Military Relations in Argentina.* University Park, Pa.: Pennsylvania State University Press.

Pion-Berlin, David, ed. 2001. *Civil-Military Relations in Latin America: New Analytical Perspectives.* Chapel Hill, N.C.: University of North Carolina Press.

Portes, Alejandro. 1995. *En Torno a la Informalidad: Ensayo sobre Teoría y Medición de la Economía No Regulada.* Mexico City: M.A. Porrúa Grupo Editorial.

Prebisch, Raúl. 1982. *La obra de Prebisch en la CEPAL. Selección de Adolfo Gurrieri.* Mexico City: Fondo de Cultura Económica.

Przeworski, Adam, Michael E. Alvarez, José Antonio Cheibub, and Fernando Limongi. 2000. *Democracy and Development: Political Institutions and Well-being in the World, 1950-1990.* Cambridge, UK: Cambridge University Press.

Psacharopoulos, George, Ariel Fiszbein, Bill Wood, Haeduck Lee, and Samuel Morley. 1997. *Poverty and Income Distribution in Latin America: The Story of the 1980s.* World Bank Technical Paper No. 351. Washington, D.C.: The World Bank.

Raboy, Marc, and Bernard Dagenais, eds. 1992. *Media, Crisis, and Democracy: Mass Communication and the Disruption of Social Order.* Newbury Park, Calif.: Sage Publications, Inc.

Rama, Germán W., ed. 1980. *Educación y sociedad en América Latina y el Caribe.* Santiago de Chile: United Nations Children's Fund (UNICEF).

Rama, Germán W. 1984. *El sistema educativo en América Latina.* Buenos Aires: Kapelusz.

Rama, Germán W., ed. 1987. *Desarrollo y educación en América Latina y el Caribe.* Buenos Aires: Kapelusz.

Ramsey, Russell W. 1997. *Guardians of the Other Americas: Essays on the Military Forces of Latin America.* Lanham, Md.: University Press of America.

Reinicke, Wolfgang H. 1995. *Banking, Politics, and Global Finance: American Commercial Banks and Regulatory Change, 1980-1990.* Aldershot, UK: Edward Elgar.

Revista de la Cepal. 2001. "Homenaje a Raúl Prebisch." No. 75 (Dec.): 7-113.

Reyna, José Luis, ed. 1995. *América Latina a fines de siglo.* México, D.F.: Fondo de Cultura Económica.

Risse, Thomas, Stephen C. Ropp, and Kathryn Sikkink, eds. 1999. *The Power of Human Rights: International Norms and Domestic Change.* Cambridge, UK: Cambridge University Press.

Roberts, Bryan R. 1995. *The Making of Citizens: Cities of Peasants Revisited*, 2nd ed. New York: Halsted Press.

Roberts, Kenneth M., and Erik Wibbels. 1999. "Party Systems and Electoral Volatility in Latin America: A Test of Economic, Institutional, and Structural Explanations." *American Political Science Review* 93 (3): 575-590.

Rodriguez, Linda Alexander, ed. 1994. *Rank and Privilege: The Military and Society in Latin America.* Wilmington, Del.: Scholarly Resources.

Rodríguez, Victoria E. 1997. *Decentralization in Mexico: From Reforma Municipal to Solidaridad to Nuevo Federalismo.* Boulder, Colo.: Westview Press.

Roett, Riordan. 1999. *Mercosur: Regional Integration, World Markets.* Boulder, Colo.: Lynne Rienner Publishers.

Rustow, Dankwart A. 1970. "Transitions to Democracy: Toward a Dynamic Model." *Comparative Politics* 2 (April): 337-363.

Rustow, Dankwart A., and Kenneth Paul Erickson, eds. 1991. *Comparative Political Dynamics.* New York: HarperCollins.

Sassen, Saskia. 1996. *Losing Control? Sovereignty in an Age of Globalization.* New York: Columbia University Press.

Schedler, Andreas. 1998. "What Is Democratic Consolidation?" *Journal of Democracy* 9: 2: 91-107.

Schmitter, Philippe C. 1991. "Cinco reflexiones sobre la cuarta onda de democratizaciones." In *Transiciones a la Democracia en Europa y América Latina,* eds. Carlos Barba Solano, José Luis Barros, and Javier Hurtado. Mexico City: M.A. Porrua Grupo Editorial.

Schoultz, Lars, William C. Smith, and Augusto Varas, eds. 1994. *Security, Democracy, and Development in U.S.-Latin American Relations.* Coral Gables, Fla.: North-South Center Press at the University of Miami.

Schuurman, Frans J., ed. 1993. *Beyond the Impasse: New Directions in Development Theory.* London: Zed Books.

Schydlowsky, Daniel M. 1995. *Structural Adjustment: Retrospect and Prospect.* Westport, Conn.: Praeger Publishers.

Scott, James C. 1972. *Comparative Political Corruption.* Englewood Cliffs, N.J.: Prentice-Hall.

Silva, Eduardo. 1998. *The State and Capital in Chile: Business Elites, Technocrats, and Market Economics.* Boulder, Colo.: Westview Press.

Smith, Peter H. 1991. "Crisis and Democracy in Latin America." *World Politics* 43 (4): 608-635.

Smith, Peter H., ed. 1993. *The Challenge of Integration: Europe and the Americas.* Coral Gables, Fla.: North-South Center Press at the University of Miami.

Smith, Peter H., ed. 1995. *Latin America in Comparative Perspective: New Approaches to Methods and Analysis.* Boulder, Colo.: Westview Press.

Smith, William C., and Roberto Patricio Korzeniewicz, eds. 1997. *Politics, Social Change, and Economic Restructuring in Latin America.* Coral Gables, Fla.: North-South Center Press at the University of Miami.

Smith, William C., Carlos H. Acuña, and Eduardo A. Gamarra, eds. 1994a. *Democracy, Markets, and Structural Reform in Latin America: Argentina, Bolivia, Brazil, Chile, and Mexico.* Coral Gables, Fla: North-South Center Press at the University of Miami.

Smith,William C., Carlos H. Acuña, and Eduardo A. Gamarra, eds. 1994b. *Latin American Political Economy in the Age of Neoliberal Reform: Theoretical and Comparative Perspectives for the 1990s.* Coral Gables, Fla: North-South Center Press at the University of Miami.

Souza, Celina. 1997. *Constitutional Engineering in Brazil: The Politics of Federalism and Decentralization.* New York: St. Martin's Press.

Spink, Peter, and Luiz Carlos Bresser-Pereira, eds. 1998. *Reforma do Estado e Administração Pública Gerencial.* Rio de Janeiro: Fundação Getúlio Vargas.

Spybey, Tony. 1996. *Globalization and World Society.* Cambridge, UK: Polity Press.

Stallings, Barbara, ed. 1995. *Global Change, Regional Response: The New International Context of Development.* Cambridge, UK: Cambridge University Press.

Stark, Jeffrey. 1998. "Globalization and Democracy in Latin America." In *Fault Lines of Democracy in Post-Transition Latin America*, eds. Felipe Agüero and Jeffrey Stark. Coral Gables, Fla: North-South Center Press at the University of Miami.

Stavenhagen, Rodolfo. 1996. *Ethnic Conflicts and the Nation-state.* New York: St. Martin's Press.

Stepan, Alfred. 1970. *The Military in Politics: Changing Patterns in Brazil.* Princeton, N.J.: Princeton University Press.

Stepan, Alfred. 1985. "State Power and the Strength of Civil Society in the Southern Cone of Latin America." In *Bringing the State Back In*, eds. Peter B. Evans, Dietrich Rueschemeyer, and Theda Skocpol. Cambridge, UK: Cambridge University Press.

Stepan, Alfred. 1988. *Rethinking Military Politics: Brazil and the Southern Cone.* Princeton, N.J.: Princeton University Press.

Stepan, Alfred, ed. 1989. *Democratizing Brazil: Problems of Transition and Consolidation.* New York: Oxford University Press.

Stiglitz, Joseph E. 2002. *Globalization and Its Discontents.* New York: W.W. Norton.

Teichman, Judith A. 2001. *The Politics of Freeing Markets in Latin America: Chile, Argentina, and Mexico.* Chapel Hill, N.C.: University of North Carolina Press.

Theobold, Robin. 1990. *Corruption, Development, and Underdevelopment.* London: Macmillan Publishers.

Thorp, Rosemary. 1992. "A Reappraisal of the Origins of Import-Substituting Industrialization, 1930-1950." *Journal of Latin American Studies* 24 (quincentenary supplement): 181-196.

Thorp, Rosemary, and Laurence Whitehead, eds. 1987. *Latin American Debt and the Adjustment Crisis.* Pittsburgh: University of Pittsburgh Press.

Tilly, Charles. 1988. "Social Movements, Old and New." *Research in Social Movements, Conflicts and Change* 10: 1-18.

Tokman, Victor E., and Guillermo O'Donnell, eds. 1998. *Poverty and Inequality in Latin America: Issues and New Challenges.* Notre Dame, Ind.: University of Notre Dame Press.

Touraine, Alain. 1964. *Social Mobility, Class Relationship and Nationalism in Latin America.* Documento de Trabajo No. 13. Buenos Aires: Instituto Torcuato di Tella, Centro de Sociología Comparada.

Touraine, Alain. 1987. *Actores Sociales y Sistemas Políticos en América Latina.* Santiago de Chile: Regional Employment Programme for Latin America and the Caribbean (PREALC).

Touraine, Alain. 1989. *América Latina: Política y Sociedad.* Madrid: Espasa Calpe.

Tulchin, Joseph S., and Allison Garland, eds. 1997. *Argentina: The Challenges of Modernization.* Wilmington, Del.: Scholarly Resources, Inc.

Tulchin, Joseph S., and Allison M. Garland, eds. 2000. *Social Development in Latin America: The Politics of Reform.* Boulder, Colo.: Lynne Rienner Publishers.

Underhill, Geoffrey R.D., ed. 1996. *The New World Order in International Finance.* London: Macmillan Publishers.

United Nations Economic Commission for Latin America (ECLA). 1950. *The Economic Development of Latin America and its Principal Problems.* Lake Success, N.Y.: United Nations Department of Economic Affairs.

United Nations Economic Commission for Latin America and the Caribbean (ECLAC). 2000. *Equity, Development and Citizenship.* Presented to the 28th session, Mexico City, April 3-7. Santiago de Chile: ECLAC.

United Nations Economic Commission for Latin America and the Caribbean. 2001. *Preliminary Overview of the Economies of Latin America and the Caribbean 2001.* Santiago, Chile: ECLAC.

United States Law. 2002. 22 U.S. Code Section 2656f(d). <http://www4.law.cornell.edu/uscode/22/2656f.html>.

Valenzuela, Arturo, and J. Samuel Valenzuela. 1986. "Party Oppositions under the Chilean Authoritarian Regime." In *Military Rule in Chile: Dictatorship and Oppositions,* eds. J. Samuel Valenzuela and Arturo Valenzuela. Baltimore: The Johns Hopkins University Press.

Valenzuela, J. Samuel. 1990. *Democratic Consolidation in Post-Transitional Settings: Notion, Process, and Facilitating Conditions.* Working Paper No. 150. Notre Dame, Ind.: Helen Kellogg Institute for International Studies at the University of Notre Dame.

Valenzuela, J. Samuel, and Arturo Valenzuela, eds. 1986. *Military Rule in Chile: Dictatorship and Oppositions.* Baltimore: The Johns Hopkins University Press.

Vellinga, Menno, ed. 1997. *The Changing Role of the State in Latin America.* Boulder, Colo.: Westview Press.

Velloso, João Paulo dos Reis, ed. 1995. *MERCOSUL e NAFTA: o Brasil e a integração hemisférica.* Rio de Janeiro: J. Olympio Editora.

Veltmeyer, Henry, and James Petras. 1997. *Neoliberalism and Class Conflict in Latin America: A Comparative Perspective on the Political Economy of Structural Adjustment.* New York: St. Martin's Press.

Ward, Peter M., and Victoria E. Rodríguez. 1999. *New Federalism and State Government in Mexico: Bringing the States Back In.* Austin, Texas: Lyndon B. Johnson School of Public Affairs, University of Texas at Austin.

Waters, Malcolm. 1995. *Globalization.* London: Routledge.

Weffort, Francisco C. 1992. *New Democracies, Which Democracies?* Washington, D.C.: Latin American Program, The Woodrow Wilson International Center for Scholars.

Weffort, Francisco C., and Aníbal Quijano. 1976. *Populismo, Marginalización y Dependencia: Ensayos de Interpretación Sociológica.* San José, Costa Rica: Editorial Universitaria.

Weintraub, Sidney, ed. 1994. *Integrating the Americas: Shaping Future Trade Policy.* Coral Gables, Fla: North-South Center Press at the University of Miami.

Weyland, Kurt. 2002. "Limitations or Rational-Choice Institutionalism for the Study of Latin American Politics." *Studies in Comparative International Development* 37: 1 (Spring).

Williamson, John, ed. 1990. *Latin American Adjustment: How Much Has Happened?* Washington, D.C.: Institute for International Economics.

Williamson, John. 1993. "Democracy and the 'Washington Consensus.'" *World Development* 21 (8): 1329-1337.

Wionczek, Miguel S. 1985. *Politics and Economics of External Debt Crisis: The Latin American Experience.* Boulder, Colo.: Westview Press.

Wong, Siu-Lun. 1988. *Emigrant Entrepreneurs: Shanghai Industrialists in Hong Kong.* Hong Kong: Oxford University Press.

World Bank. 1992. *World Development Report 1992.* New York: Oxford University Press.

World Bank. 1997. *World Development Report 1997: The State in a Changing World.* Washington, D.C.: The World Bank.

World Bank. 2001. *World Development Report 2000/2001: Attacking Poverty.* Oxford, UK: Oxford University Press.

World Bank. 2002. "2001 World Development Indicators" Washington, D.C., at <http://www.worldbank.org/data/wdi2001/pdfs/tab4_2.pdf>.

World Bank. 2002. *World Development Report 2002: Building Institutions for Markets.* Washington, D.C.: The World Bank.

World Social Forum. 2001. Porto Alegre, Brazil, at <http://www.forumsocial-mundial.org.br>.

World Social Forum. 2002. Porto Alegre, Brazil, at <http://www.forumsocial-mundial.org.br>.

Yoffie, David B. 1983. *Power and Protectionism: Strategies of the Newly Industrializing Countries.* New York: Columbia University Press.

AUTHORS

Manuel Antonio Garretón M. is Professor of Sociology at the Universidad de Chile and has been a visiting professor at universities in Europe, the United States, and Latin America. He studied at the Universidad Católica de Chile and received his doctorate from l'Ecole des Hautes Etudes in Sciences Sociales in France. He is the author of numerous books and articles on politics, culture, and society in Chile and in Latin America. He is the author of *Política y Sociedad entre dos época. América Latina en el cambio de siglo* (Homo Sapiens, 2000); *La Sociedad en que vivi(re)mos. Introducción sociológica al cambio de siglo* (Ediciones LOM, 2001); and *The Incomplete Democracy* (University of North Carolina Press, forthcoming 2003); and coeditor of *Democracy in Latin America: (Re)constructing Political Society* (United Nations University Press, 2001).

Marcelo Cavarozzi is Dean of the School of Politics and Government of the Universidad Nacional de San Martín in Buenos Aires, Argentina. He has been a visiting professor at Yale University, Georgetown University, the Massachusetts Institute of Technology, and the University of North Carolina at Chapel Hill. He received his Ph.D. in Political Science from the University of California, Berkeley, and has published widely on politics in Latin America. He is the coeditor of *El Asedio a la Política: Los Partidos Latinoamericanos en la era neoliberal* (Homo Sapiens, 2002); and the author of "Transitions: Argentina, Bolivia, Chile, and Uruguay," in *Democracy in Latin America: (Re)constructing Political Society* (United Nations University Press, 2001).

Peter S. Cleaves is Executive Director of AVINA, the Swiss foundation for sustainable development in Latin America and the Iberian Peninsula. He has served as Professor of Government and Director of the Institute of Latin American Studies at the University of Texas, the Ford Foundation Representative for Mexico and Central America, and Vice President of the First National Bank of Chicago. He received a B.A. from Dartmouth College, an M.A. from Vanderbilt University, and a Ph.D. in Political Science from the University of California, Berkeley. His publications include *Bureaucratic Politics and Administration in Chile* (University of California Press, 1974); *Agriculture, Bureaucracy and Military Government in Peru* (Cornell University Press, 1980); and *The Professions and the State: The Mexican Case* (University of Arizona Press, 1987).

Gary Gereffi is Professor of Sociology at Duke University. He received a B.A. from the University of Notre Dame and a Ph.D. in Sociology from Yale University. He has published extensively on international business, regional economic integration, and national development strategies in various parts of the world. He is the author of *The Pharmaceutical Industry and Dependency in the Third World* (Princeton University Press, 1983); and the coeditor of *Manufacturing Miracles: Paths of Industrialization in Latin America and East Asia* (Princeton University Press, 1990); *Commodity Chains and Global Capitalism* (Praeger Publishers, 1994); *The Value of Value Chains: Spreading the Gains from Globalisation* (special issue of the *IDS Bulletin* 32: 3, July 2001); and *Free Trade and Uneven Development: The North American Apparel Industry after NAFTA* (Temple University Press, 2002).

Jonathan Hartlyn is Professor of Political Science at the University of North Carolina at Chapel Hill. He received a B.A. from Clark University and an M.Phil. and Ph.D. in Political Science from Yale University. He has published extensively on the comparative politics of Latin America, especially with relation to questions of democratization, political institutions, and state-society relations. He is the author of *The Struggle for Democratic Politics in the Dominican Republic* (University of North Carolina Press, 1998) and *The Politics of Coalition Rule in Colombia* (Cambridge University Press, 1988); coauthor of "Democracy in Latin America Since 1930," *Cambridge History of Latin America*, Vol. VI, Part II (Leslie Bethell, ed., 1994); and the coeditor of several books, including *Democracy in Developing Countries: Latin America*, 2nd ed. (Lynne Rienner Publishers, 1999).

INDEX